God & Jesus Loves You I Love You God bless you   John 3:16
Have a blessed day every day
God bless Ishael Jews Jerusalem   watch For
Pray for peace of Jerushwa   knprture
Pray For Ishaeli Jews Jerusanla   Shalom
Iant W 49   10-7-2022

        I Love You   many hugs From me to you

Rooted in God 2

            Dr Render
        i f you give This book awny
            to Anyone
        keep the Sinnese
                Prayer in this book
        thanks,
            Appreciate it

D1065779

Carolyn E. Hoth

Rooted in God 2

DECODING BIBLE PLANTS FOR 21ST CENTURY LIFE

§

Dr. Carolyn A. Roth

Carolyn Roth Ministry

Published in the United States of America
Publisher: Carolyn Roth Ministry, www.CarolynRothMinistry.com
ISBN 9781946919014
ISBN: 1946919012
Religion / Bible Studies /
Religion / Biblical Commentary / General 14.04.21

Dedication

To my husband, Bruce Roth

Acknowledgements

§

THE FOLLOWING INDIVIDUALS PROVIDED SUPPORT as I prepared this book:

Dr. Elaine Solowey, Arava Institute for Environmental Studies, Ben Gurion University at Kibbutz Ketura, spent valuable time with me when I studied in Israel. She reviewed plants and aspects of Judaism.

Sara Gold, www.wildflowersinIsrael.com/, for the many photographs and expert consultation.

Contents

Introduction

§

LIKE US, PLANTS GROAN UNDER the impact of sin in the world. They wait in eager expectation for a new earth to be revealed. Most people are unaware that the Bible mentions over 125 different plants. Yet, Holy Scriptures contain no excess information or "filler." Every scripture is given by God and is valuable for instruction in holy living. Whether a fruit tree, grain, or thistle, each Bible-identified plant has a purpose in Bible stories.

In *Rooted in God 2*, you read how Bible characters interacted with plants. We can learn, or refused to learn, Godly lessons from Bible plants.

Rooted in God 2 is a reformation of *Rooted in God* (2014). *Rooted in God* was enormously popular; however, *Rooted in God 2* is even better. I used reader's feedback to improve the book. A major change is integration of plant photographs in the narrative. Another change is clear application of Bible plants to twenty-first century Christian life.

Approach this book by reading Bible reference(s). Then, read the story synopsis. Study the meaning and use of each plant to ancient people. Look at plant pictures. Contemplate the Reflection and apply it to your busy life. End each chapter by working through questions and activities in Unifying Thoughts.

CHAPTER 1

Garden of Delight

§

ON DAY 3 OF CREATION, God caused the dry land to appear on earth and spoke plants into existence. God said, "Let the land produce ... seed bearing plants and trees" (Ge 1:11 niv). Plants include trees, shrubs, herbs, bushes, grasses, vines, ferns, mosses, and flowers. Initially, there were no plants on the dry land because there was no man to work the ground (Ge 2:5). God's earliest plan was for man and plants to interact, i.e., man to tend plants and plants to give food to man.

God intended Adam to have a different relationship with animals than with plants. He gave Adam dominion, supreme authority, or absolute ownership over animals. In contrast, God told Adam to tend, guard, and keep the garden and its plants. God entrusted plants to mankind. What an awesome responsibility!

Currently, most of us don't need to grow vegetables and fruits. We can buy them in stores and markets; yet, many of us have gardens. There is joy in enriching the soil and nurturing seeds to full growth. We delight to see our own flowers grow and bloom, crave succulent fruits from our trees, and yearn to stimulate taste buds with fresh-grown herbs. There is something inherently satisfying about gardening.

Gardening instincts shouldn't surprise us. Our spiritual father, God, was a gardener, the producer of all vegetation on the earth. Gardening is in our genetic makeup. Unlike Adam and Eve, most of us don't live in a delightful garden; however, God's plan is for us to live with plant creation. God wants all vegetation, i.e., brightly colored flowers and leafy trees, to delight our eyes and soothe our spirits.

As you read this chapter, think about God's original plan for the earth, its plants, and mankind. Then, reflect on changes God made to each of these—earth, plants, man—as a result of Adam and Eve's choice to disobey him.

BDELLIUM OUTSIDE EDEN (GENESIS CHAPTER 2)

God planted the Garden of Eden east of Israel, probably near the Tigris and Euphrates Rivers in Iraq. The Hebrew word for Eden is *êden*, which means "delight."[1] The Garden of Delight was a place of pristine natural beauty; all manner of plants grew there. A river ran through Eden and watered it. After leaving Eden, the river formed the head waters of the Pishon, Gihon, Tigris, and Euphrates Rivers. The Pishon River wound through the land of Havilah, noted for its gold and bdellium, an aromatic resin. The bdellium tree was the first plant identified in the Bible.

The bdellium tree (*Commiphora africana*) is native to sub-Saharan Africa. Probably, it didn't grow in Israel. Ancient Egyptian women carried small bdellium-filled pouches as perfume. The Hebrew word for bdellium comes from *bâdal*, which means "to separate, divide, or distinguish from."[1] The bdellium tree symbolized the separation between the Garden of Eden and outside lands. Eden included plants for beauty and food; it was all sufficient. In contrast, the land of Havilah was noteworthy only for its gold and one tree, the bdellium.

Living in Jesus is like living in Eden. With Jesus our lives are beautiful, fertile, and satisfying. When we are separated from him, that is, outside of Eden, our lives are bland and unproductive. Often, we hunger for something that isn't present. That something is Jesus and a life lived with him.

Reflection: St. Paul assured Christians that nothing can stop Jesus from loving us. What stops, or separates, us from loving him?

Was it A Real Tree? (Genesis chapter 2)

God placed numerous plants in the Garden of Eden; however, he is recorded as naming only two: The Tree of Knowledge of Good and Evil and the Tree of Life. We don't know who named the other plants. Possibly, God named each plant as he named each star. Alternatively, God may have allowed Adam to name plants like Adam named animals and birds.

When God placed Adam in the Garden of Eden, he told Adam not to eat from the Tree of Knowledge of Good and Evil. God was explicit: the penalty for eating from this tree was death. Adam understood that death meant his body would cease to be alive. God wouldn't have given Adam such a crucial command unless he was sure Adam fully understood it.

Adam knew which tree God meant when he said the Tree of Knowledge of Good and Evil. The tree was located near the center of Eden, was attractive to the eye, and produced fruit that looked good to eat. When God questioned Adam and Eve after they ate from the Tree of Knowledge of Good and Evil, neither responded with, "I didn't know which tree you meant."

The words God used in Ge 2:17 are noteworthy. God declared: *when*, not *if*, you eat of the Tree of Knowledge of Good and Evil, you will die. "When" means in the time that something is done or comes about. Even when God forbid Adam from eating Tree of Knowledge fruit, he knew Adam would disobey him.

Inside and outside of the Judeo-Christian community, the Tree of Knowledge of Good and Evil generates much discussion. Was it a real tree or a symbol of mankind's movement from innocence to awareness of sin? If a real tree, what fruit did it produce?

Answers to these questions come from climate data, history, and Bible dictionaries. When the Tree of Knowledge was described in the Bible, the Hebrew word *êts* was used for tree. [1] This word was used for tree approximately 25 places in Genesis and the Old Testament. In each use, *êts* referred to a distinct tree, not to an abstraction such as morals, conscience, or judgment.

Many of us grew up believing the Tree of Knowledge of Good and Evil was an apple tree and the fruit an apple. This is unlikely because the Garden of Eden was probably located between the Tigris and Euphrates Rivers in Iraq. The Iraqi plain is arid, soil is sandy, and annual rainfall is about 13 inches. Apple trees thrive best in temperate climates and in deep, well-drained, loam soil. They need 39-49 inches of rain fall annually, distributed over the growing season. On the Iraqi plain, annual precipitation and soil composition didn't favor growth of a succulent apple that would tempt Adam and Eve.

Recently, commentators proposed that the Tree of Knowledge of Good and Evil was a pomegranate tree, an apricot tree, a fig tree, a date palm tree, and even the grape vine. None of these suggestions is consistent with the Hebrew language in which the Garden of Eden story was first told and later written. The Hebrew language has a word for each proposed tree and the grape vine, i.e., the word for both the pomegranate tree and its fruit is *rimmôn*.[1] If the Tree of Knowledge was one of these trees, the Genesis author would have recorded the tree's common name.

I believe that the Tree of Knowledge of Good and Evil was a unique tree. Because modern botanists haven't determined its species is no reason to conclude the Tree of Knowledge of Good and Evil didn't exist.

The Tree of Knowledge of Good and Evil symbolized moral knowledge and the ability to make ethical choices. Moral knowledge is about principles of right and wrong and includes treating others with respect, doing good, and acting justly. Adam and Eve came from the hand of God. Initially, they possessed God's moral knowledge and ideas of right and wrong.

In contrast to God's standards of morality, human perceptual and psychological morality are finite, even flawed; they change as society's values change. Today, individuals often say that God's moral precepts changed since Eden; that God adjusted his expectations as mankind's conscience evolved. That is a human, self-centered view that discounts Holy Scriptures which asserted that both God and his purpose are unchangeable (Mal 3:6; Heb 6:16-17).

Reflection: Think about the source of your morality. Are you living by your own morality, society's morality, or God's morality?

CONCEALING FIG LEAVES (GENESIS CHAPTER 3)

Originally, mankind was created with free will. Adam and Eve could choose to obey or disobey God. While they obeyed God, they lived sinless lives. In their innocence, neither Adam nor Eve wore clothes. They were naked in each other's presence and God's presence; yet, they felt no shame or embarrassment.

Everything changed when Adam and Eve disobeyed God and ate fruit from the Tree of Knowledge of Good and Evil. They lost their sinless state and their innocence. It was Adam and Eve's choice to disobey God, more than the act of biting into, chewing, and swallowing a fruit, which introduced sin into the world.

After eating fruit from the Tree of Knowledge, Adam and Eve were aware they were naked. Adam was embarrassed for Eve to see his naked body; likewise, Eve was embarrassed for Adam to see her body. To hide their nakedness, Adam and Eve sewed fig leaves together and made aprons to cover themselves. The Hebrew word for apron is *châgôrâh*, which means "belt." [1] Fig leaves are rough and hairy on the underside. When injured, they exude a sticky, milky fluid. Fig leaves felt rough and sticky against Adam and Eve's skin.

Adam and Eve wore fig leaf aprons when they tried to avoid God as he walked in the garden in the cool of the day. In God's presence, Adam blurted out, "I was afraid because I was naked; so I hid" (Ge 3:10 niv). In reality, Adam wasn't naked; he was wearing a fig leaf apron. In Adam's mind, the fig leaf apron was adequate to cover his nakedness/shame in front of Eve, but not in front of God.

Fig trees (*Ficus carica*) are native to the Middle East where they produced two crops of figs annually. June figs were a delicacy and eaten fresh, while August figs were dried and used during the winter or on long trips. Dried figs can be stored six-to-eight months. For ancient people, they were a good source of nutrients over winter when few plants produced fruits or vegetables.

Today, wearing clothes is the norm. We dress for the day soon after getting out of bed. I don't know about you; but, I want to look good to others. I want to present myself as a person who is attractive physically, psychologically, and spiritually. Yet, I'm not always like that. Sometimes I am a mess spiritually and other times I have enough psychological baggage to fill my closet.

Worse than projecting an idealized picture to others, I try to project this picture to God. Do you ever disobey God and then lie to him about it? I do, when I attempt to obscure my true motives from God or spin my disobedience so that I look good. What an amazing waste of time! God knew me before the world was created and when I was in my mother's womb. He knows the number of hairs on my head. God knows my true motives.

Reflection: God provided a mechanism to remove the consequences of our sin. What was it?

Thorns and Thistles (Genesis chapter 3)

After Adam and Eve sinned, the world, including plant life, became subject to death. Because of Adam's disobedience, God cursed the ground. No longer was Adam the caretaker of a sumptuous garden and its produce. Henceforth, Adam toiled (worked, sweated) to raise vegetables and grow fruit trees to feed his family. As Adam and his offspring plowed and planted crops, some native plants became weeds. The most troublesome weeds were thorns and thistles.

Thorns and thistle are the bane of any gardener. Thorns tend to be woody plants with sharp, rigid spines. Often branches are modified into leafless points. Thistles can be showy with round or tubular flowers; however, they are prickly. Today, Holy Lands have more than 100 species of thorns and thistle.

Scholars don't know which thistle grew first when Adam tilled the soil. Three are associated with the Genesis record: milk thistle, globe thistle, and Spanish century thistle. The milk thistle (*Silybum marianum*), called St. Mary's thistle, is wide-spread around the projected locations of the Garden of Eden. Pilgrims to Israel see milk thistle growing along highways and in construction sites. My friend who lives in a kibbutz in the Negev Desert area said that they use milk thistle seeds to flavor bread.

In the Genesis record, the symbolism for thorns and thistles is consequences. Consequences are the direct outcome of an action or its end-result. Adam and Eve's disobedience resulted in consequences to the earth, to their lives, and to their livelihood.

What would have happened if Adam and Eve (as a couple) discussed possible consequences of eating from the Tree of Knowledge of Good and Evil before they took the first bite of its fruit? Perhaps, they would have gone ahead and eaten the fruit; but, perhaps they wouldn't have eaten it.

Reflection: Why do we do things that we know are going to have negative consequences?

THE TREE OF LIFE LIVES (GENESIS CHAPTERS 2, 3; REVELATION CHAPTER 22)

The Tree of Life was located near the center of the Garden of Eden along with the Tree of Knowledge of Good and Evil. Although God told Adam not to eat from the Tree of Knowledge, he gave no prohibition against eating fruit from the Tree of Life. Because all trees were attractive to the eye and/or good for food, likely Adam and Eve ate fruit that grew on the Tree of Life.

After Adam and Eve's disobedience, God reflected on their newfound knowledge: "The man has now become like one of us, knowing good and evil. He must not be allowed to reach out his hand and take also from the tree of life and eat and live forever" (Ge 3:22 niv).

Adam and Eve's access to the Tree of Life was based on a proper relationship with God. When that relationship was severed, so was their access to the life-giving tree. To prevent Adam and Eve from eating tree-of-life fruit, God expelled them from the Garden of Eden. He placed cherubim on the east side of the garden. The cherubim had flaming swords that flashed back and forth and blocked Adam and Eve's access to the Tree of Life.

The Garden of Eden was destroyed before or during the flood of Noah's time when the topography of the land was changed; however, the Tree of Life wasn't destroyed. Rather, God moved it. The Tree of Life is in paradise (Rev 2:7) and is destined to return to earth. In the New Jerusalem, a river will flow from the throne of God, down the middle of a great street (Rev 22:1-2). The Tree of Life will be located on both sides of the river. Each month it will produce a different variety of fruit. Christians who are victorious in overcoming evil will be able to eat fruit from the Tree of Life.

When the Bible referred to the Tree of Life, the Hebrew word for life was *chay*. *Chay* means "alive or living thing." [1] Life is contrasted with death. This same word, *chay*, was used when God breathed into Adam's nostrils the breath of life and Adam became a living being. Both man and plants live; they breathe, grow, reproduce, and die. Originally, man and plants were to live forever; however, both were corrupted by man's sin.

Because Adam and Eve disobeyed God, they forfeited eternal physical life; but, they didn't forfeit God's love and care. Even though God banished Adam and Eve from the Garden of Eden, he remained their father. He continued to interact with them and their offspring. God made a way for Adam and Eve's offspring to be reconciled to him and regain eternal life.

Reflection: Take time to reflect on your life. Are you living the "alive life" that God planned for you here on earth?

UNIFYING THOUGHTS

As I read the creation story, I wondered why God created plants before he created the sun. Plants require light to produce food and give off oxygen. If the sun was created first, the process of plants preparing the earth for man's habitat would have moved quicker. Intuitively, I wanted to reverse days three and four of creation to make the creation process more efficient.

Then, I laughed at myself, remembering God's words: "For my thoughts are not your thoughts, neither are your ways my ways, declares the Lord. As the heavens are higher than the earth, so are my ways higher than your ways and my thoughts than your thoughts" (Isa 55:8-9 niv).

God didn't need my input into the creation process. He exists separate from my perspective on time. God didn't care if creation took millions of years. It is I, with a limitation of about 80 years to live, who wants to hurry things along. When Adam and Eve disobeyed God, they thought their knowledge was superior to God's. The result was that sin and death entered the world.

1. If you were in the Garden of Eden, would you have acted differently than Adam and Eve? How? What would have been some results of your actions?

2. Did you ever make plans for God, rather than let him make plans for you? How did that go? Knowing what you know now, would you have done anything differently?

3. Think about submitting your will and life to God. Thoughtfully, list five areas in your life that you want to submit. What are the advantages and disadvantages of submitting each of them? What actions could you take to submit more of your life to God?

4. Do you think Adam and Eve ate from the Tree of Life from the time they were created until the time God expelled them from Eden? Why or why not?

5. Re-read and think about the implications of Isaiah 55:8-9. Consider memorizing the two verses so you can recite them when you evaluate your goals and plans.

CHAPTER 2
Early Fathers

§

CHAPTER TWO HIGHLIGHTS PLANTS IN the lives of five Bible patriarchs: Noah, Abraham, Isaac, Jacob, and Joseph. This Bible lore comes from Genesis. As you read about plants in the lives of the ancient fathers, think about how they are integral to the story. Ponder the meaning of each plant, i.e., immortality, superstition. Draw parallels between the plant in the life of the ancient father and your life.

NOAH'S CYPRESS WOOD ARK (GENESIS 6:9–8:22)

Noah was over 500 years-old when God told him to build an ark, a giant water-proof vessel. The ark's purpose was to save Noah, his family, and animals from a flood that would destroy the world. Noah was chosen because he was righteous, blameless among the corrupt and violent people of his time. The Bible doesn't identify where Noah lived. After the flood, the ark landed on Mount Ararat. Today, Mount Ararat is in the Republic of Armenia in the Middle East.

Noah built the ark from wood and coated it with pitch inside and out to help it float. The ark's dimensions were 450 feet long, 75 feet wide, and 45 feet high. It was rectangular shaped. Most of us remember seeing pictures of the ark from childhood Bible story books. In those books, the front (prow, bow) of the ark was pointed. Sometimes, the back (stern) was pointed or narrower than sides of the ark. Likely, the ark didn't have a prow or stern because it didn't plow through the water in a specific direction, nor was it steered by a rudder. Instead, the ark was built to float on the top of the water and to withstand the impact of rain and floods.

After gathering the animals into the ark, Noah and his family entered it. Seven days later, rain started. From the deep earth, springs of water burst forth. Many Christian scholars believe that the flood was turbulent and included movement of the earth's tectonic plates resulting in massive tsunami floods. The ark's occupants remained safe in the ark for almost a year.

Botanists aren't 100% sure which tree Noah used to build the ark. Earth's landscape was altered by the great flood and some plant species destroyed. Several Bibles recorded that Noah used cypress wood, also called gopher wood, (*Cupressus sempervirens*). The Hebrew word *gôpher* means cypress.[1]

Cypress trees are large, strong, durable, and full of resin. Resins are organic substances secreted by plants that are insoluble in water. Resin kept flood water from seeping into the wood and sinking the ark. Cypress wood has a distinctive, strong odor, described as warm, pungent, and male-like. Possibly, the cypress odor helped offset the smell of all those animals in the ark.

The cypress wood ark carried eight individuals through the raging flood that destroyed life in the known world. Not surprisingly, the cypress tree was associated with immortality through God's divine will. In the upward tip of the columnar-shaped cypress tree and in every shoot and leaf, cypress branches and needles point to immortal life with God.[2]

Receiving the gift of immortality from Jesus doesn't absolve men and women from acting right (or righteously). Instead, Jesus calls us to a new life, which includes a new way of thinking and behaving. The Bible gives direction on how we should live our mortal lives. The Bible is our "self-help" book and points the way to God and immortality.

Reflection: How are you planning for your immortality by actions here on earth?

Oaks of Mamre (Genesis 14:13, 18:1-8)

When Abraham was about 75 years-old, God told him to leave his home in Haran. Abraham traveled with his wife Sarah, nephew, Lot, and servants to Canaan. Eventually, Lot separated from Abraham because their flocks became large. Abraham moved to the great trees of Mamre near Hebron.

The great trees of Mamre were most likely Palestinian oaks (*Quercus calliprinos*). The Palestinian oak is the most common tree found in Israel's landscape. At one time, it was an important hardwood for ships, ploughs, and yokes. Bark was a source of tannin to dye skins and leather. Acorns were roasted and eaten during famine. The warlike tribe, Dan, made "way-bread" from acorns to take to war.

In the Bible oaks were associated with power, strength, and longevity in the sense of long life. The great oaks of Mamre symbolized Abraham's long life. A Palestinian oak near Hebron, named Abraham's Oak, is thought to be over 850 years-old.

God promised that he will be with his servants through life, even into their old age and gray hairs (Ps 71:18). Christians don't have to worry about what they will do in retirement. They can use Abraham as their role model. God called Abraham to a new adventure when he was 75 years-old. Abraham lived 175 years. Following Noah's death, only Isaac lived longer than Abraham.

An Israelite proverb is that the fear of the Lord adds length to life; but the years of the wicked are cut short (Pr 10:27). Perhaps, the underlying logic of this proverb is as simple as individuals who fear the Lord live more prudent lives than do the wicked; therefore, they live longer. Whatever the proverb's immediate cause and effect, it is in God's Word and we can use it to guide our lives.

Reflection: Is having a long life important to you? How do you think a long life is related to fear of the Lord?

Entangled in a Thicket (Genesis 22:1-19)

Isaac was the son that God promised Abraham and Sarah; the son through whom the Messiah would come. When he was about 16 years-old, God commanded Abraham to take Isaac to Mount Moriah and sacrifice him as a burnt offering. Abraham didn't hesitate or question God's command. Early the next morning, Abraham, Isaac, and two servants started walking toward Mount Moriah.

When they reached Mount Moriah, Abraham built an altar, arranged wood on it, and tied Isaac on top of the wood. Abraham picked up his knife, prepared to slay Isaac. At the last minute, an angel told Abraham not to kill Isaac. The angel commended Abraham for fearing God enough to be willing to sacrifice his son.

Abraham looked up and saw a ram caught by the horns in a nearby thicket. The ram was simply there, waiting for Abraham to see it. The thicket held the ram in place in much the same way that Isaac's bindings held him on the altar. Abraham killed the ram and offered it to God as a burnt offering.

A thicket is a group of wild shrubs and occasional small trees which grow together to form impenetrable branches and roots. In thickets trees rarely grow more than 10-20 feet tall. Often shrubs have thorns and vines entangled with them. The chaste tree, prickly juniper, and myrtle could have been part of the Mount Moriah thicket. In present day Israel, controlled plants, i.e., flowers and domesticated trees, have replaced thickets except where cultivated land was abandoned.

The Hebrew word for thicket comes from the word *çâbak*, which means "to entwine in the sense of inter-woven branches."[1] In English, entanglement means "to twist together and to ensnare." Often entanglements cause confusion. Imagine the confusing thoughts that Satan brought to Abraham's mind during the three-day walk to Mount Moriah; i.e., "Surely God doesn't mean for you to sacrifice Isaac? A God that really loved and cared about you would never require you to kill your beloved son."

In contrast to the ram entangled in the thicket, Abraham didn't become entangled in Satan's lies or become confused by his limited understanding of God or by the situation. Abraham obeyed God, believing that God would keep his promise and Isaac would be the father of nations.

Reflection: Think about a time when you were twisted, or entangled, in a problem. How did you involve God?

MANDRAKE SUPERSTITION (GENESIS 30:14-22)

Jacob married two sisters. His first wife was Leah. His second was Rachel, Leah's younger sister. Jacob loved Rachel more than Leah. At the time of this story, Leah had birthed four sons, but stopped conceiving children. Rachel had no children even though Jacob spent his nights with her.

When Leah's son brought mandrakes to his mother, Rachel asked Leah for them. Resentful of Jacob's preference for Rachel, Leah refused to give the mandrakes to her sister. Rachel proposed a trade. Jacob will spend the night with Leah in return for Leah giving Rachel the mandrakes. Leah agreed and gave the mandrakes to Rachel.

Many ancient people superstitiously believed that mandrakes promoted fertility and conception in barren women. Women ate small amounts of mandrake root, cut them into an amulet to wear, or put them under the marriage bed. Both Rachel and Leah wanted children and believed that mandrakes could help them conceive a child. Rachel wanted children to validate herself as a woman. Leah wanted additional children to secure Jacob's affection. As a result of the night Jacob spent with Leah, Leah conceived a fifth son. Rachel didn't become pregnant despite obtaining mandrakes.

The mandrake (*Mandragora officinarum*) is native to lands around the Mediterranean Sea including ancient Canaan. The root is the notable part of the mandrake and most often associated with fertility and conception. Mandrake roots are large and brown, similar to parsnips. They grow three-to-four feet and weigh several pounds. Frequently, the thick root is forked and reminds viewers of two legs. In modern Israel mandrake plants are rare.

The Bible story of Jacob's wives and mandrakes showed they were superstitious. Before we are too critical of these two women, think about the number of individuals who read their horoscope daily. Believing that mandrakes promoted conception and that a horoscope foretells type of day a person will have are both attempts to circumvent God's will.

Reflection: Why aren't you willing to let God handle all your problems? Why do you act superstitiously?

DREAM OF REEDS (GENESIS 41:1-40)

Jacob and Rachel's first son was Joseph. Joseph's life was influenced by his dreams and the dreams of others. He alienated his brothers by telling them his dream where they bowed to him. Because of their jealousy, Joseph's brothers sold him into slavery.

Joseph became a slave in Egypt. Later he was sent to prison. There, Joseph developed a reputation for interpreting dreams. The king of Egypt, pharaoh, had a dream. He sent for Joseph to interpret it.

The dream showed pharaoh standing on the Nile River bank. He saw seven, sleek, fat cows emerge from the river and graze among the reeds. Then, seven, ugly, lean cows came out of the river. The ugly, lean cows ate the sleek, fat cows, but remained ugly.

In pharaoh's dream reeds were most likely the Egyptian common reed (*Phragmites australis*). In ancient Egypt, this reed was used to control soil erosion. Wild animals lived among and ate reeds. Poor Egyptians used reeds to build houses and weave mats, nets, and ropes. The Egyptian reed was used as a measuring rod. Because Joseph interpreted pharaoh's dream, pharaoh made Joseph the second-most powerful man in Egypt.

Reeds symbolized corporal, or material, truth and knowledge.[2] Corporal truth is little more than opinion. It changes with cultural norms and personal experiences. In contrast, divine truth is eternal and unchangeable. God is the God of truth; his teachings are true and unchangeable. God's truths are seen primarily in the Bible.

Reflection: Divine truth is a measuring rod we can use to evaluate our thoughts, beliefs, and behaviors.

Unifying Thoughts

Plants breathe. Plant breathing is a busy process where sugars and starches are converted into energy so new plant tissue is built. In Chapter 2 the men and women were busy. They used a lot of energy building, traveling, tending flocks, and rearing children. Most of their efforts were congruent with God's will. Generally, they used their energy wisely.

1. Consider where Christians would be now if Noah hadn't built the ark? If Abraham didn't leave Haran? If Esau was the ancestor of the Messiah? If Rachel didn't give birth to Joseph?

2. If you were Noah's wife or sons, what would you have thought when Noah started to build a giant ship? How would you have supported/not supported him?

3. List the top five ways you spend energy. Consider that using energy is not synonymous with amount of time spent. Now record five ways that you would like to spend your energy.

4. Questions for consideration about your answers:

   - How much of the original energy expenditure was for God?
   - How much of the revised energy expenditure will be for God?

5. Read Col 1:28-29. You can use these verses to evaluate how to use your energy in the future.

Challenges of Moses

§

THE LIFE OF MOSES COVERS four Bible books: Exodus, Leviticus, Numbers, and Deuteronomy. Moses was born in Egypt where the Israelites were slaves. He was a prophet, leader, and intermediary between God and the Israelites. Chapter 3 describes five plants significant in Moses' life. Sometimes I think that Moses was a botanist. He included not only the names of many plants, but their uses and growth patterns. The symbolism, or meaning, of these plants enhances our understanding of God and his interactions with the Israelites. Importantly, plant meaning and symbolism have application to twenty-first century Christian life.

A BULRUSH CRADLE (EXODUS 1:1–2:10)

Jacob and his family (70 members) settled in the Goshen area of Egypt around 1876 BC. Moses was born about 350 years later. In the interim, the Israelites became numerous and heavily populated Goshen. A new pharaoh came to power in Egypt who didn't know the history of Joseph saving Egypt. Threatened by the number of non-Egyptians living in his country, pharaoh made the Israelites slaves. Then, to reduce the Israelite population, pharaoh ordered that every Israelite male infant be thrown into the Nile River to die.

When Moses was born, his mother, Jochebed, determined to keep him alive. She crafted a cradle from bulrushes and coated it with a tar-like substance to make it water proof. Jochebed placed Moses in the cradle and set it among Nile River reeds. Moses' sister, Miriam, guarded the cradle.

Jochebed made the bulrush cradle from a stately aquatic reed, the Nile papyrus (*Cyperus papyrus*). The papyrus reed is native to countries around the Mediterranean Sea. In ancient Egypt, bulrushes were a source of paper and used to make pens, boxes, baskets, mattresses, and boats.

The Hebrew word for bulrush comes from the word *gâmâ*, which means "to absorb."[1] When something is absorbed, it is taken in and made part of the existing whole. Moses' cradle was made of porous bulrushes which absorbed air. The air allowed the bulrush cradle to float.

When we accept Jesus as savior, we become members of the body of Christians. Ideally, we affiliate with and are absorbed into a local body of believers. Being absorbed into a local body of believers requires intention. First, we need to find other Christian believers. Most often we find them in a church. Second, we need to open ourselves to these Christians so we can absorb the Christ-likeness in them. Third, we need to willingly give the Christ-in-us to others.

Reflection: Within the body of Christians, there is room for individual differences. We are free to be ourselves as we interact with fellow believers.

God in a Bush (Exodus 3:1-22)

From when he was weaned through age 40, Moses lived in royal splendor as the son of pharaoh's daughter. Despite his privileged life, Moses knew he was an Israelite and his people were slaves. As an adult, Moses went to a site where Israelites worked as slave laborers. He saw an Egyptian overseer beating an Israelite. Moses killed the overseer. Shortly afterward, pharaoh ordered Moses killed for his crime.

To escape pharaoh's wrath, Moses fled Egypt and traveled to Midian. Midian was east of the Sinai Peninsula and outside Egypt's influence. In Midian, Moses met Jethro and married his daughter, Zipporah. He became a shepherd for his father-in-law. After about 40 years, Moses led the sheep west, arriving at Mount Horeb on the Sinai Peninsula.

Near Mount Horeb Moses saw a burning bush. Looking closer, Moses noticed that the bush wasn't consumed by the fire. Deciding to investigate the strange phenomenon, Moses walked toward the bush. When he neared it, God called from within the bush and ordered Moses to come no closer. God instructed Moses to take off his sandals because Moses was standing on holy ground. The bush that Moses saw is thought to be the blackberry (*Rubus sanctus*), often called the sacred blackberry.[3]

God introduced himself to Moses, naming himself the God of Abraham, Isaac, and Jacob. God told Moses that the Israelites were suffering severely under the Egyptian slave masters. God planned to rescue the Israelites from the Egyptians and lead them to a land of milk and honey.

Probably, Moses was nodding his head and agreeing with God's every word. Then, God stunned Moses by saying, "So now, go. I am sending you to Pharaoh to bring my people the Israelites out of Egypt" (Ex 3:10 niv). Immediately, Moses started questioning his qualifications to be the leader God described. God's response was to continue telling Moses to go to Egypt.

The sacred blackberry plant is a symbol of God revealing himself to man. Reveal means "to make known something that was secret or hidden." In the Old Testament nowhere does God reveal more about himself to a man than in the burning bush story. God revealed:

- God remembered the promises he made to Moses' ancestors 400 years earlier. God doesn't forget
- God heard the cries of Israelite slaves in Egypt. God isn't limited to a single country or geographical area, i.e., Canaan
- God knew and cared about Abraham's offspring. He cares about his people over centuries and millennia
- God had a defined plan to free the Israelites from slavery in Egypt. God is a God of specifics
- God knew that pharaoh would oppose him; however, the gods of Egypt were powerless against him. God is the one true God

Most Christians and many non-Christians want to know more about God, the Father. Jesus told his followers that if they wanted to know the Father, they should look at the words and behaviors of the Son. Jesus did his Father's will in all things.

Reflection: God, who is all powerful, knowledgeable, and present, claims each of us as his child. Have you accepted God's claim on you?

BITTER HERBS IN PASSOVER (EXODUS 11:1 – 12:36)

When Moses returned to Egypt, he asked pharaoh to allow the Israelites to go into the desert and worship God. Pharaoh's answer was an emphatic "No." Pharaoh wasn't about to allow valuable slaves to leave Egypt. Because of pharaoh's prideful, stubborn, and manipulative behavior, God visited ten plagues on Egypt.

The tenth and final plague was named "The Plague of the Firstborn." This plague caused the death of the firstborn of every man and animal in Egypt, except those of the Israelites. To keep the death angel from entering Israelite homes, God directed them to slaughter a lamb or goat and place the animal's blood on the sides and top of their door frames. The meat was roasted and eaten with bitter herbs and unleavened bread.

In Egypt, bitter herbs included endive, chicory, dandelion, sow thistle, and wild lettuce. The bitter herb used in the first Passover meal varied among families. Nothing green remained on trees or plants after the locust plague (eighth plague). Consequently, some families had one type of bitter herb, while other families had a different type.

Endive (*Cichorium endivia*) is an example of a bitter herb. Many early Bibles translated bitter herbs as endive. The origin of endive is lost from history. The endive leaf grows in crowded circles or in spirals from the plant center. Leaves are about six inches-long and bright green. An Israeli colleague said they make coffee from endive root.

The symbolism of bitter herbs, including endive, is clear from the name, i.e., bitterness. Bitterness is something intensely distressing or disturbing to the mind, an expression of severe pain, grief, or regret.

Originally, a free people living in Egypt, the Israelites became bitter when they were enslaved by the Egyptians. They were worked brutally to make bricks, plant and harvest crops, and build irrigation systems. The Israelites felt excruciating bitterness when their sons were murdered by Egyptians.

God told the Israelites to eat bitter herbs at the Seder meal to remind themselves of their bitterness in Egypt. In contrast, Paul told the Ephesian congregates to rid themselves of bitterness (Eph 4:31). How do we reconcile Paul's instruction to put off all bitterness with God's direction to the Israelites to remember their bitterness in a meal?

Reflection: Is there a difference between remembering a bitter occasion as a precursor to celebrating a better life versus remembered bitterness that leads to resentment of situations, people, and God?

Healing Mangrove at Marah (Exodus 15:23-27)

Events that preceded the episode at Marah included the Israelite exodus from Egypt and the destruction of pharaoh's army. Now, the Israelites were safe from pursuit and ready to head for the Promised Land!

Moses led the Israelites southeast from the Red Sea into the Desert of Shur on the Sinai Peninsula. For three days, the Israelites traveled through the desert until they reached Marah. There, they expected to find fresh water. Instead the water was bitter and undrinkable. The Bible doesn't disclose how the water was bitter; but, it could have contained high concentrations of salt. If the Israelites drank the salty water, they would become dehydrated and die.

By the time the Israelites reached Marah, they were hot, foot sore, and feeling the effects of an adrenaline let down after their escape from Egypt. They realized that they were in the desert and had no homes. They had no secure food source. Now, the water was undrinkable. Not surprisingly, the Israelites grumbled, asking each other "What are we going to drink?" Moses asked the same question. The difference between the Israelite community and Moses was that Moses turned to God about the problem of drinkable water.

God answered Moses by showing him a piece of wood. He told Moses to throw the wood into the bitter water. The result was that the bitter water became sweet. In this passage, the Hebrew word for sweet is *'mâthaq*, meaning "to relish." The water turned sweet in the sense of drinkable.

The gray mangrove (*Avicennia marina*) tree could have produced the wood used by Moses at Marah.[4] Among mangrove species (eight-or-nine), the gray mangrove is both a pioneer and a relict. Pioneer because it will be the first mangrove species that populates an area. Relict because it remains in an area after other mangrove species are extinct. In brackish water, salt enters mangrove trees through roots and bark. Salt is concentrated in leaves and in tree bark.

Gray mangrove wood illustrated God's assurance that he would heal the Israelites. At Marah, the Israelites were only three days out of Egypt with generations of slavery behind them. Perhaps, many believed they were no more than property, their opinions worthless, and they couldn't care for themselves. God was more than willing to heal them from these negative self-images. In fact, God wanted to make them into a nation that would capture and occupy the Promised Land.

Reflection: We have a choice to grumble or to turn to God for healing. Which do you do?

COMPLAINT ABOUT ONIONS (NUMBERS 11:4-34)

Once the Tabernacle was built and dedicated, the Israelites resumed their journey to the Promised Land. After traveling three days, the community started to complain about food. The complaints began with people the Bible called, "the rabble." The rabble was largely non-Israelites who joined the Israelite exodus so they could scape Egypt. Hearing the rabble complain, some Israelites joined in. The complaints included:

- if only we had meat to eat
- we remember the fish, cucumbers, melons, leaks, onions, and garlic we ate in Egypt
- we never see anything but this manna
- we have lost our appetites for manna

The vegetables identified in Nu 11:5 were the most extensive list of vegetables in the Bible. They were eaten in Egypt, not Canaan. Often vegetables available in Egypt and Israel weren't the same plant species. In this Bible passage, the onion is the Egyptian walking onion (*Allium cepa*). This species grows from off-sets (bulbs) rather than seeds.

Egyptians believed that spheres of the universe, i.e., heaven, earth, and hell, were concentric circles similar to the layers of an onion cut in half at the diameter.[5] In contrast, Israelites believed that God formed the visible universe from what was invisible. Christians know that Jesus (the Word) spoke the universe into existence.

In this episode, the onion symbolized complaints or complaining. The universe, or at least earthly society, would run smoother if individuals stopped complaining. Despite knowing the sovereignty of God and his Son in creation, Christians are like ancient Israelites in their penchant for complaining. Writing to the church at Philippi, Paul cautioned Christians not to complain or argue (Php 2:14-16). If Christians have a complaint against one another, they are to forgive the person just as Jesus forgave them (Col 3:13).

Reflection: How can you "Delete the Complaint" button in your mind!

UNIFYING THOUGHTS

Chapter 3 showed Moses and the Israelites on the move. Moses went from Egypt to Midian and back to Egypt. The Israelites traveled on the Sinai Peninsula. The Lord led the Israelites with a cloud pillar by day and a fire pillar by night. They moved when the pillars move; thus, they traveled at God's command. Often, we think plants are stationary, but they are in constant motion. Translocation is the process of water, minerals, and food moving through a plant's vascular system to growth and storage areas, such as roots.

1. Whether we move across town or thousands of miles, how can we ensure that we move at God's will?

Moses and the Israelites moved at God directed, but God also moved: "For the Lord your God moves about in your camp to protect you and to deliver your enemies to you. Your camp must be holy, so that he will not see among you anything indecent and turn away from you" (Dt 23:14-15 niv).

God moved throughout the Israelite camp! Similarly, God moves around our homes and in us. Just as Moses admonished the Israelites to make sure that God didn't see anything indecent in their camp, it's important that God not see anything indecent in our homes or in us.

2. In your home, what don't you want God to see?

3. Do you have thoughts that you think are private and no one knows? The Holy Spirit knows.

4. Reflect on God's goodness to you. Do you have food, shelter, and safety? What could you complain less about?

5. How do you think God feels when you complain?

Building a Tabernacle

§

THE NEWLY-FREED ISRAELITES ARRIVED AT Mount Sinai about three months after leaving Egypt. Mount Sinai is located in an arid, mountainous region in the southcentral Sinai Peninsula. There, the Israelites constructed the Tabernacle and dedicated it in early 1445 BC. The Tabernacle consisted of two parts: the Tent of Meeting and a surrounding Courtyard. At the Tent of Meeting, God spoke with the Israelites. In the Courtyard, sacrifices were made to God. Chapter 4 contains five plants associated with the Tabernacle. Each plant depicts God's relationship with the Israelites. Many point toward the future Messiah's relationship with his followers.

WOOD FOR THE TABERNACLE (EXODUS CHAPTERS 25, 35 - 38)

Acacia was the only wood used in Tabernacle construction. The Tent of Meeting walls were built of gold-covered acacia wood panels (boards). In the Tent of Meeting, the Table of the Presence Bread (Showbread), the Altar of Incense (Golden Altar), and the Ark of the Covenant were built from acacia wood and overlaid with gold. Gold-covered acacia wood posts and cross bars stabilized the wood panels and held the Tent of Meeting curtains in place. Gold-covered acacia wood poles were inserted in gold rings on the four corners of the Table of the Presence Bread, Altar of Incense (Golden Altar), and Ark of the Covenant (Testimony). Poles were used to lift and carry each piece of furniture.

In the Courtyard, acacia wood poles and posts held linen curtains in place. The Altar of Burnt Offering was built from acacia wood overlaid with bronze. Bronze-covered acacia wood poles were inserted into brass rings to carry the Bronze Altar.

When the Israelites moved from one camp to another, the Tent of Meeting and Courtyard were deconstructed. Levites carried the Tent of Meeting and sacred furniture on their shoulders. Acacia wood is beautiful, light, and practically indestructible. It was ideal for the multiple moves the Israelites made in their 40-year journey on the Sinai Peninsula and final march into Canaan.

The Bible identified the wood used to build the Tabernacle as *shittâh*, which translates as acacia.[1] Most likely it was red acacia (*Acacia seyal*). The tree is native to the dry, desert-like climate of the southern Sinai Peninsula. The red acacia grows where annual precipitation is as low as nine inches. Two gray straight thorns grow at the base of each leaf. In the Sinai Desert, the acacia tree's yellow flowers bloom July through December. Ancient people used acacia wood to build furniture; while leaves and stems were used for animal fodder.

In the Tabernacle, acacia wood symbolized the indestructability of Jesus. Isaiah described the coming Messiah as "a root out of dry growth" similar to the acacia tree growing out of arid, desert soil (Isa 53:2). Acacia wood is virtually indestructible; however, Jesus is fully indestructible. The indestructible Jesus rose after death and sits at God's right hand in heaven. Burnt offerings on acacia wood altars are no longer needed for sins to be forgiven and individuals reconciled to God. With his death and resurrection, Jesus completed the reconciliation process once and for all.

As Christians, we are God's workmanship, created to do good works which God prepared for us to do (Eph 2:10). How indestructible depends on how much effort we make to stay close to Jesus. The best ways to stay close to Jesus are by regular, preferably daily, Bible reading, prayer, and meditation on the Holy Scriptures.

Reflection: Most of us would like our epitaph to read: " _(your name) was indestructible in his/her walk with Christ." How can you start today to make that epitaph true for you?

Linen Curtains (Exodus chapter 26)

In the Tent of Meeting, a linen curtain called the Veil hung between the Holies of Holy and the Most Holy of Holies. The Tent of Meeting roof was made of linen curtains that draped over the outside of the gold-covered acacia wood panels. Cherubim, made from purple, blue, and scarlet yarn, were embroidered on the Veil and woven into the roof curtains. The entrance to the Tent of Meeting (east side) was a linen curtain woven from blue, purple, and scarlet yarn.

The Tabernacle Courtyard was rectangular, 150 feet on the north and south sides and 75 feet on the east and west sides. The sides were made of non-dyed linen curtains. At the Courtyard entrance, the curtain was made from blue, purple, and scarlet yarn.

Tabernacle linen came from the flax plant. The Hebrew word for Tabernacle linen is *shêsh*. *Shêsh* means "fine linen" and denoted a type of Egyptian linen of peculiar whiteness and excellence.[1] Fine linen was soft and flexible, yet strong and cool to wear. It had a luster, or sheen, that made it look like silk. In ancient Egypt, fine linen was a mark of quality and associated with wealth and rank.

As slaves in Egypt, the Israelites didn't have much, if any, fine linen; however, when they left Egypt, the Egyptians gave them tribute. The tribute included clothes and more than likely fine linen and yarns. When Moses asked the Israelites for offerings to build the Tabernacle, he specified the need for fine linen and colored yarn.

Linen is made from the flax plant (*Linum usitatissium*). Flax grew in Egypt from the fifth millennium before the birth of Christ (BC). Flax grew along the Nile River and in the Nile Delta region. It was planted in late fall or early winter and harvested in spring. Dry flax stalks were soaked (retted) to separate flax fibers from the woody tissues. Egyptians dyed some flax. Blue and purple dyes came from shellfish, while scarlet dye was harvested from worms that lived on evergreen oak trees.

In Revelation, St. John used "clean, shining linen" as a symbol for purity. Purity means "spotless, stainless, and free from what pollutes" including moral fault or guilt. In the Tabernacle, animals were sacrificed and blood shed to accomplish ritual purification. Today, purity involves actively pursuing faith, love, and peace. It means we are free from moral guilt in the way we think about and act toward others.

Keeping a pure heart is intentional and ongoing work. Because we don't always remain pure in thoughts, words, and actions, God made a way for us to reconcile ourselves to him and his purity. If we confess sins to God, he will cleanse us and purify us from unrighteousness (1Jn 1:9). Having a pure, clean heart is as simple as going to God, agreeing with him about our sins, and asking his forgiveness.

Reflection: When did you last agree with God about your own sins?

WATCHING ALMONDS (EXODUS 25:31-40, 37:17-24)

In the Tabernacle, an almond tree design appeared on the Lampstand. The Lampstand and its accessories were made of 75 pounds of gold. The Lampstand stood in the Holy of Holies on the south side of the room, opposite the Table of the Presence Bread. It was one solid piece of hammered gold.

The height and width of the Lampstand weren't identified in the Bible; however, its base and arms were described in detail. Three branches extend from one side and three branches from the opposite side of a central base and stem. Along each of the six branches were three cups shaped like almond flowers with buds and blossoms. Likely, the central lamp stem set on the fourth almond blossom where the stem connected with the base. Today, Christians and Jews refer to similar-shaped Lampstands as "menorah."

The Tabernacle almond tree is the common almond (*Prunus amygdalus*). Almond trees grew throughout Canaan. When Jacob directed (circa 1875 BC) his sons to go to Egypt to buy grain, he told them to take almonds as a gift to the Egyptians. Almonds were one of the best products of Canaan. Ancient people ate almonds raw or roasted. Almonds flavored porridge, breads, and pastries. They were pressed for oil. A flowering almond tree is one of the most beautiful sights in nature.

In the Hebrew language, the name for the almond tree is *shâqêd*, from a primary root meaning "to be on the lookout and watchful."[1] The almond tree symbolized watchfulness because of its early flowering. On the Lampstand, almond buds pointed to the constant watchfulness of God and the need for Israelites to watch their own behavior to ensure they kept God's commandments.

God's watchfulness over Israel extended beyond the Tabernacle. Job referred to God as "a watcher of men" (Job 7:20). After showing Jeremiah a vision, God asked Jeremiah what he saw (Jer 1:11-12). Jeremiah responded that he saw the branch of an almond tree. God replied that Jeremiah saw correctly. God was watching to see that his word was fulfilled in Israel.

Reflection: God watches to see that his will, word, and work are fulfilled in each of us. Do you watch yourself?

An offering of Wheat (Leviticus chapter 2, 24:5-1)

In the Tabernacle, the bread loaves were called the Presence Bread or the Showbread. The Presence Bread was made with finely ground wheat flour, olive oil, and salt. The bread was baked the day before the Sabbath, one loaf for each of the 12 tribes of Israel. Each Sabbath, new loaves were set out before the Lord on the Table of the Presence. The Presence Bread was placed in two piles of six loaves. The loaves removed from the Table were eaten by the priests. In most early societies women baked bread; however, men (Kohathites) from the tribe of Levi baked the Presence Bread. The bread was unleavened, that is, made without yeast

The earliest wild wheats were einkorn and emmer. Wheat was domesticated prior to 7000 BC in Asia Minor and the Nile Delta. In the Bible, the first reference to wheat was about 1900 BC in Paddan Aram; Jacob's son, Reuben, returned from the fields during the wheat harvest. Israeli botanists believe that ancient Israeli wheat was emmer.

Today, in the Middle East, most wheat is common wheat (*Triticum aestivum*), known as bread wheat. In Israel's Jezreel Valley, farmers grow fields of wheat (see photograph in Chapter 2 for wheat growing in a Jezreel Valley field in front of cypress trees). For Israelites, wheat symbolized life, primarily physical life, from God. God named wheat first among the seven species of plants Israelites would find in the Promised Land (Dt 8:8). Ancient peoples called wheat the "giving grain" and associated it with the cycle of life and death.

I am intrigued that God told the Israelites to bake bread every week out of wheat. Why didn't God allow them to use manna for the

Presence Bread? Manna was plentiful and God provided a steady supply of it. Instead, God required the Israelites to make an offering from wheat, a grain difficult to access during their 40 years on the dry Sinai Peninsula.

Reflection: Think about your last challenging task. Why does God give us hard "stuff " to do?

THE OLIVE TREE'S ROLE (EXODUS 27:20-21, 30:22-24)

Olive trees were identified three places in the Tabernacle. In each place, olive oil rather than olives or olive wood was used. First, olive oil provided fuel for the seven lamps which set on the Golden Lampstand. The seven oil lamps were the only source of light in the Tent of Meeting. Second, olive oil was an ingredient in the Presence Bread. The third way olive oil was used in the Tabernacle was as an ingredient in the oil used to anoint or consecrate the Tabernacle furniture and the Israelite priests.

The olive tree originated in present day Israel and Syria. Probably, olive trees (*Olea europaea*) were first domesticated in the fourth millennium BC. Olive trees grew in the Sinai Peninsula when the Israelites journeyed there in 1446-1406 BC.

In Israel, the oldest olive trees are in the gardens adjacent to the Church of all Nations on the Mount of Olives. Visitors are kept from touching these cherished trees by rod iron fences. Olive trees live up to 1000 years. The current Mount of Olive trees could be as few as two-to-three generations from the olive trees on the Mount of Olives when Jesus walked there.

Hebrew word for olive tree, olive, and olive oil is *zayith*. *Zayith* means "yielding illuminating oil."[1] Repeatedly, Old Testament psalmists told the Israelites that God was their light. In turn, the Israelites were to reflect God's light to the surrounding nations.

Remember the song we learned as children? It went something like this:

This little light of mine, I'm going to let it shine.
This little light of mine, I'm going to let it shine.
This little light of mine, I'm going to let it shine.
Let it shine. Let it shine. Let it shine.

Reflection: Is your life shinning for Jesus where you work and relax?

Unifying Thoughts

Plants eat and drink. Absorption is the process by which substances, i.e., minerals and water, move into plants. Primarily, absorption occurs through plant roots, but sometimes through leaves. Although the Tabernacle was the outward sign of God to the Israelites, the root of the Israelites faith was God. God was the ultimate food and water for the Israelites.

Jesus, the Christ, is our Presence Bread; however, unlike the Tabernacle Presence Bread that was baked and rotated weekly, Jesus, the bread of life, died once for all of us. Once we accept him into our lives, he doesn't rotate in and out. He stays!

Jesus said: "Unless you eat the flesh of the Son of Man and drink his blood, you will have no life in you. Whoever eats my flesh and drinks my blood has eternal life and I will raise him up at the last day" (John 6:53-54 niv).

1. What life was Jesus referring to when he said that a requirement for life is eating his flesh and drinking his blood? Life here on earth? Life in heaven?

2. Is eating Jesus' flesh and drinking his blood as simple taking Communion or was Jesus talking about a different action? Perhaps, an additional activity?

3. If you aren't sure where you will be spending eternity, ponder these Bible verses:

   • Romans 3:23
   • Romans 6:23
   • John 3:16

Removing original sin from our lives and having eternal life is as simple as believing in Jesus, the Son of God.

4. Most of us want to reflect Jesus in our lives. List three ways to rid yourself of any dullness and better mirror Jesus in your life.

CHAPTER 5
Life in the Promised Land

§

CHAPTER 5, LIFE IN THE Promised Land, focuses on the Israelites entering, conquering, and living in Canaan. This time span was about 350 (1406-1050 BC) years and described in the books of Joshua, Judges, and Ruth. This Bible section begins with God appointing Joshua leader over the Israelites. Joshua administered the division of the Promised Land to the 12 tribes.

A tiny boundary point was named after the henbane plant. After Joshua died, judges proclaimed God's will to the Israelites. Judges included Deborah, Gideon, and Samson. Plants associated with them were the palm tree, thistle, and yitran. The book of Ruth is a snapshot of everyday life in the Promised Land, including the barley harvest.

HENBANE INTOXICATION (JOSHUA CHAPTERS 13 - 21)

Joshua encouraged Israel's faithfulness to God, commanded the military, and divided the Promised Land among the 12 tribes. On the west side of the Jordan River, land was distributed by lot. Once assigned land, tribes were to settle and retain their land.

In the Promised Land, some regions and cities were named after plants. An example is Shikkeron, (also called Shicron), named after the henbane plant. Shikkeron was a point on the boundary between the tribes of Judah and Dan. It wasn't listed as a town that Judah or Dan inherited; perhaps, it was a small village or merely an identifiable site.

The Israeli golden henbane (*Hyoscyamus aureus*) is from a family of plants which includes potatoes, tomatoes, and chili peppers. Henbane originated in the Mediterranean region of Asia Minor. In the Egyptian *Ebers Papyrus* (circa 1550 BC), henbane was identified as a medicinal herb used for sedation and pain relief. Pilgrims can see henbane growing between stone cracks on the Western (Wailing) Wall in Jerusalem and between stone blocks in ancient monasteries.

Shikkeron comes from the Hebrew word *shikkârôwn*, which means "intoxication or drunkenness."[1] What an unfavorable name for such an attractive little plant! I'd prefer to associate henbane with something positive such as hope for the future in the Promised Land or obedience to God in conquering and holding a tiny place.

Intoxicate means "to excite or stupefy," by alcohol or a drug, to the point where physical and mental control is reduced or lost, i.e., drunkenness. Perhaps, the henbane plant's name was a warning to the Israelites that they shouldn't get overly excited or drunk on their success in conquering the Promised Land. God gave them the land. Now, they needed to be good stewards of its bounty.

In the first century through the twenty-first century, God gives Christians the same advice as he gave Israelites who entered the Promised Land: Don't become so over-excited or stupefied by alcohol that you are seduced from duty whether to God or your spouse (Eph 5:18). Not getting drunk is a principle for Godly living over millennia.

Reflection: Do you ever become so intoxicated over your successes that you forget to give credit to God? How can you start giving credit where credit is due?

Deborah's Palm Tree Court (Judges chapters 4, 5)

Deborah was both a prophetess and a judge in Israel for 40 years. As a prophetess, Deborah heard messages from God and transmitted them to the Israelites. She held court (judged) under a palm tree called the Palm of Deborah in Ephraim.

Today, palm trees (*Phoenix dactylifera*) are distributed widely in Israel even in the Negev Desert where trees are irrigated. Palm trees look like an umbrella. They have a long trunk and leaves only grow from tree tops. Palm dates are the fruit of the palm tree. Most palm trees produce dates for well over 100 years.

When God described the Promised Land to Moses, he called it a land of milk and honey. Contrary to popular belief, most honey wasn't produced by bees. Honey was syrup preserved from the palm date or reduced from the sap of palm tree flowers. Date syrup is almost black and has the consistency of molasses or sorghum.

Over millennia, the palm tree and its branches represented peace, elegance, majesty, and military triumph. Juxtaposition to these concepts is the way the palm tree fits into Deborah's life. For Israelites of Deborah's time, the palm tree signified justice. Deborah held court under the palm tree and distributed justice.

God expected Israelites to act justly, i.e., not treat the poor differently from the rich. The prophets exhorted the Israelites to do right, seek justice, and encourage the oppressed. The Israelites even had proverbs that addressed justice. One proverb was: "When justice is done, it brings joy to the righteous but terror to evildoers" (Pr 21:15 niv).

Reflection: How can you show justice in your various roles and duties today at work, to your spouse, with your children?

Punishing Thorns (Judges 8:1-21)

Gideon acted as a judge over Israel between 1162-1122 BC. At that time, the Midianites were Israel's primary enemy. The Midianites were marauders who swarmed across the Promised Land stripping the land bare of grains, fruits, and vegetables. When Gideon and 300 men routed a massive force of Midianites, some of them fled east across the Jordan River.

In pursuit of the Midianites, Gideon and his men came to the Israelite town of Succoth. There, Gideon requested bread for his worn-out men; however, Succoth officials insolently refused to give him provisions. Possibly, they weren't sure that Gideon would defeat the Midianite kings and feared reprisal from them. Gideon was angry at the town leaders. He promised to return and punish them.

At Karkor, Gideon and 300 men defeated 15,000 Midianite soldiers and captured their kings. Returning from battle, Gideon caught a young man of Succoth and learned the names of the 77 Succoth officials. Then, Gideon went to Succoth and seized them.

Thorns and briers were a common method of punishment in the ancient world. They were placed on a man's naked body and pressed down by heavy implements, often a heavy wooden sleigh. The sleigh was dragged back and forth over the individual's body so thorns and brier spines dug deep into and tore the skin. Given the officials very public and insolent refusal to assist Gideon's hungry men, soldiers enthusiastically applied this punishment to Succoth elders.

Most likely, Gideon used the Syrian thistle (*Notobasis syriaca*). In Israel and east of the Jordan River in lands claimed by the Israelites, the Syrian thistle is widespread. Today, the Syrian thistle is found in disturbed lands in the same habitats as milk thistle (Chapter 1). Syrian thistles appear similar to milk thistles. They have no beneficial uses.

In the episode between Gideon and the Succoth officials, the Syrian thistle symbolized retribution. Retribution means "dispensing or receiving" reward or punishment. Retribution is often confused with revenge. Revenge which means "to avenge oneself usually by retaliating in kind," i.e., an eye for an eye. Although retribution and revenge have some of the same characteristics and synonyms, retribution includes justice. Gideon exacted retribution (justice), not revenge, on the Succoth officials.

Reflection: Think about a time when you wanted retribution. Could you have really wanted revenge?

Ruth Gleaned Barley (Book of Ruth)

Naomi and her daughter-in-law, Ruth, left Moab and returned to Bethlehem during the spring barley harvest. To make bread Ruth went into harvested fields and picked (gleaned) grain heads left in fields after farmers reaped them. Ruth gleaned in fields owned by Boaz, a wealthy kinsman of Naomi's husband. Boaz encouraged Ruth to remain in his fields where she would be safe. Ruth gleaned in Boaz's fields until the barley and wheat harvests were completed and threshing started.

While grain was threshed, Boaz slept on the threshing floor. One night. Naomi instructed Ruth to go to the threshing floor and after Boaz was asleep to lie at his feet. Ruth followed Naomi's instructions. During the night Boaz woke, found a woman at his feet, and inquired who she was.

Ruth identified herself and told Boaz that he was a kinsman-redeemer. A kinsman-redeemer was the nearest male relative of a widow's deceased husband. The kinsman-redeemer had the responsibility to marry the widow. Subsequently, Boaz married Ruth. Although a Moabite, Ruth was the great grandmother of King David and an ancestress of Jesus.

Domesticated barley (*Hordeum vulgare*) was grown in the Middle East from about 7,000-6,000 BC. Barley was a major food staple for several reasons. First, it was less expensive to purchase than wheat. Second, barley was drought-resistant and grew in the diverse habitats of the Promised Land. Third, under favorable growing conditions, barley ripened in as few as 60-70 days. Barley was the flour of poor Israelites. Derogatorily, the Midianites referred to Israelites as "loaves of barley" (Jdg 7:13-15).

Barley is synonymous with first fruits. It's the first grain to mature in a new year. Israelites demonstrated thanks for the harvest by taking a sheaf of the first barley harvested to the priests. The priest waved the barley sheaf before God in thanks for the harvest. Once the "wave sheaf "was offered to God, barley could be harvested throughout the community.

God named the Israelites the first fruits of his harvest; while Christians are the first fruits of the Holy Spirit (Rom 8:23). Israelites demonstrated thanks for the harvest by giving the first sheaf of harvested barley to God. Similarly, Christians give God the first fruits of their time, talent, and treasury.

Reflection: God's commandment to give him our first fruits was designed so that he could shower blessings on us (Mal 3:10).

SAMSON'S TIED WITH YITRAN (JUDGES CHAPTERS 13 – 16)

Samson lived in the original tribal lands of Dan and was a judge over Israel for 20 years (1075-1055 BC). From conception Samson was a Nazirite, which meant both Samson's mother and Samson abstained from grape products, didn't cut his hair, nor touch a dead body. When Samson was a judge, the Philistines oppressed Israel for 40 years.

From adulthood until his death, Samson achieved single-handed triumphs over the Philistines. Although Samson was an Israelite judge, his personal life was a tragedy. Samson's downfall was his preference for immoral women.

One of Samson's lovers was Delilah. In exchange for a large sum of money from the Philistine leaders, Delilah agreed to disclose the source of Samson's amazing strength. After much cajolery from Delilah, Samson told her if he was tied with seven fresh thongs (braided rope), he would become as weak as other men. Eagerly, the Philistines brought Delilah seven fresh thongs.

As Samson slept, Delilah tied his hands. With Philistines hidden in an adjoining room, Delilah cried out, "Samson, the Philistines are upon you" (Jdg 16:9 niv). Samson snapped the thongs and killed attackers. Clearly, Samson gave Delilah false information about the source of his strength.

The noted Israeli botanist, Nogah Hareuveni,[3] proposed that the ropes used to tie Samson's wrists were made from the yitran plant (*Thymelaea hirsute*) plant. The Philistines knew the strength of seven braided ropes of yitran; thus, accepted that binding Samson with them was a way to defeat his strength.

The symbolism for yitran is strength. No Bible character had more physical strength than Samson. God is our strength and shield. Psalmists recorded that God is the origin of individual strength and no warrior escapes by his own great strength. God promised that he gives strength to the weary and increases the power of the weak (Isa 40:28-29). These verses sound like being weak is good if we depend on God for strength.

Reflection: Have you ever felt spiritually strong? To what would you attribute that feeling of strength?

Unifying Thoughts

Oh, how the Israelites longed to reach the Promised Land! They could hardly wait to feel the soil beneath their feet. God promised the new land would be watered by streams and pools. What a bounteous plant-filled land God gave his children. The problem was that just like Satan corrupted Adam and Eve in the Garden of Delight, Satan corrupted the Israelites in the Promised Land by causing them to worship Canaanite idols.

1. Before we shake our heads and marvel at the degenerate hearts and behavior of the Israelites, we need to evaluate our own behavior in lavish western society. List your top three idols, being very honest. Do you worship security, money, your career, etc.?

2. Do we find ourselves mirroring the behavior of the Israelites by going our own way and doing what is right in our own eyes? Then, when we get into messy situations, we ask God to get us out? Write down a time that you did just that. How did it turn out?

3. Go back to your list of top three idols. Would you like God to forgive you for worshipping these idols? Before you say "Yes" or

"No," write out specifically what you will do to release these idols from your life. Asking God to forgive us for idol worship has little value, if we continue to worship the idols.

(4.) Reread and think about Bible stories of the three judges: Deborah, Gideon, and Samson. How were they different? Develop a "take away" message contrasting their characteristics.

CHAPTER 6

Early Israelite Monarchy

§

KEY FIGURES IN THE EARLY Israelite monarchy were Samuel, King Saul, and King David. When the Israelites requested a king, Samuel warned them that a king would take their best produce and would change their destiny. Nonetheless, the Israelites demanded a king, so God made Saul the first king of Israel. In a military campaign, Saul camped under a pomegranate tree.

King David was the best-known and loved of all Israelite kings. As a young man, David killed Goliath in the Valley of Elah (terebinth trees). We remember King David's humility as demonstrated by his prayer to be cleansed with hyssop. When King David fled Jerusalem, rather than risk a possible confrontation with Prince Absalom, his household ate beans.

SAMUEL'S WARNING (1 SAMUEL CHAPTER 8)

Samuel (born 1105 BC) was a priest, a prophet, and the greatest judge in Israelite history. Samuel's life was at the intersection of two points in time in Israel's history: when Israel was a theocracy and judges conveyed God's will to the people versus when an earthly king ruled Israel. Samuel was about 65 years-old when the Israelite leaders came to his home at Ramah. They asked for a king.

Samuel wasn't happy that Israel's leaders wanted a king. He was hurt, perceiving that the Israelites rejected his judgeship. Despite these feelings, Samuel took the leaders' request to God. God assured Samuel that the leaders weren't rejecting Samuel; they were rejecting him. God directed Samuel to warn them of the cost of having a king rule over them.

Following God's direction, Samuel identified ways a king would tax the Israelites, to include taking the best of their vines. Samuel warned them that eventually they would become the king's slaves. When this happened, the Israelites would cry out to God, but God wouldn't answer them. Disregarding Samuel's warnings, the Israelites continued to ask for a king. Again, Samuel took their demands to God. God's answer was, "Listen to them and give them a king" (1 Sa 8:22 niv).

The plant that illustrated Samuel's message to the Israelites was the grape vine (*Vitis vinifera*). Grape vines were a principle crop in ancient Israel. Currently, grape vines grow primarily in the northern and central portions of Israel. Grape vines and vineyards were mentioned over 500 times in the Bible. At times, the vine referred to peace and prosperity. At other times, it was associated with the Israelites and their destiny as God's chosen Old Testament people. Destiny is a predetermined course of events.

The author of Ecclesiastes averred that the same destiny, death, overtakes all men (Ecc 9:3, 7, 12). Because we don't know when our death will occur, we should enjoy life. Enjoying life is good; but, the destiny of Christians is life beyond death. Our destiny is a mansion in heaven with Jesus. We don't know when our death will occur; therefore, we should enjoy life. In the joy and abundance of our current lives, we must remember God, lest we give up out eternal destiny in heaven.

Reflection: Spend some time reflecting on your destiny. Are you where you want to be? What changes do you want to make?

SAUL AT A POMEGRANATE TREE (1 SAMUEL 13:16 - 14:23)

During Saul's reign, the Philistines were a persistent enemy of the Israelites. In one battle, the Philistines were camped north of the Micmash

Pass. Saul and 600 Israelites were camped south of the pass under a pomegranate tree on the outskirts of Gibeah.

God caused an earthquake and the entire Philistine army panicked and fled. Saul pursued the Philistines. Israelites, hidden in the Ephraim hills, joined the pursuit. The battle ended with the conclusion, "So the Lord rescued Israel that day" (1 Sa 14:23 niv).

The pomegranate tree's botanical name (*Punica granatum*) means a many-seeded apple. Both flower and fruit are a brilliant orange-red color. In Israel pomegranate trees were plentiful in the second millennium before Christ. The pomegranate was one of the seven plant species that Israelites found in the Promised Land. In modern day Israel, pomegranate trees grow throughout the country to include the extreme southern desserts where trees are irrigated.

In ancient Israel, it was customary for leaders to camp and/or hold court under trees. Because King Saul camped under a pomegranate tree, 3000 years ago pomegranate trees could have grown larger than they grow today. Alternatively, this pomegranate tree was taller than normal; thus, it was a well-known location.

The Hebrew word for pomegranate tree and fruit comes from *râmon*, which means "to exalt" or "lift up."[1] Perhaps, Saul had "exalt" in mind when he camped under the tree. As the first king over Israel, he knew his behavior and choices were scrutinized by supporters and detractors alike.

By camping under a tree that meant "exalt," subtly, Saul reminded the Israelites that God exalted him to the position of king.

In contrast to Saul's action, Christian's are told to humble themselves before God, then God will exalt them (Jas 4:10). God has lifted, or wants to lift, each of us out of the despair and the draining numbness of our daily lives. God wants us to live exposed to him, his purpose, and his will for our lives.

Reflection: How can you live so that you continually exalt God with your life?

Valley of Elah (1 Samuel chapter 17)

In the Valley of Elah, the Philistines prepared for battle with the Israelites. The Philistines' champion was Goliath, a giant over nine-feet tall who wore bronze armor. Goliath demanded that an Israelite champion meet him in battle. When the Israelites saw Goliath, they were terrified. No soldier or leader dared to meet Goliath in individual battle.

David's three brothers served in Saul's army. David's father, Jesse, sent David with food for the brothers and their commander. When David heard about Goliath's challenge, he asked, "Who is this uncircumcised Philistine that he should defy the armies of the living God?" (1 Sa 17:26 niv). David told King Saul that he battled bears and lions with his sling-shot while tending his father's sheep. He would accept Goliath's challenge.

The valley of Elah received its name from terebinth trees (*Pistacia terebinthus*) growing there. The Hebrew word *êlâh* refers to *Pistacia*.[1] Terebinth trees are resilient. They grow from seeds and from tree cuttings; they resprout even when cut back to the trunk. Terebinth trees live as long as 1,000 years. In present day Israel, terebinth trees grow in the Valley of Elah near a dry stream bed with plenty of flat stones for a sling shot.

The Palestinian terebinth tree symbolizes both might and knowledge of right and wrong.[2] Although these meanings have value, in the valley of

Elah, the tree is better associated with the word "solitary." Solitary means occurring singly or going alone. In the ancient Middle East, terebinth trees rarely grew in groves or groups. They grew alone. Similarly, David went out to meet Goliath alone, without companions.

Accepting Jesus is a solitary act. As individuals, we make the decision to accept or not accept him. No one, not our parents, spouse, or children, can make that decision for us. We are responsible for our own actions in this life.

Reflection: Do you remember the old American folk hymn, "Jesus Walk this Lonesome Valley?" Please read the words to this hymn and reflect on how they apply to your life:

Jesus walked this lonesome valley. He had to walk it by Himself; O, nobody else could walk it for Him. He had to walk it by Himself.

We must walk this lonesome valley. We have to walk it by ourselves; O, nobody else can walk it for us. We have to walk it by ourselves.

You must go and stand your trial. You have to stand it by yourself, O, nobody else can stand it for you. You have to stand it by yourself.

David Cleansed with Hyssop (2 Samuel 11: 1-12 – 12:25; Psalm 51)

One spring, King David remained in Jerusalem when the Israelite army went out to fight the Ammonites. Unable to sleep, David walked on the palace roof. Looking down he saw a beautiful woman, bathing. The woman was Bathsheba. She was the wife of Uriah, one of David's elite fighting men who was out of Jerusalem fighting the Ammonites. David had Bathsheba brought to him. They had intercourse. Later, Bathsheba sent David a message saying she was pregnant. Attempting to cover his transgression, David ordered Uriah placed without support in the front lines of a battle. Uriah was killed. Soon thereafter, David married Bathsheba.

David wrote Psalm 51 after the prophet Nathan confronted him with his adultery and murder. David asked God for mercy and to wash away his sins. Specifically, David asked God to cleanse him with hyssop, or rid him of all disease. David's disease was his sin of adultery and murder.

The hyssop (*Origanum syriacum*) that David referenced was the aromatic Syrian hyssop, called wild marjoram. The hairy surfaces of hyssop leaves and branches hold liquids well; thus, it was adopted as a sprinkling device. In Old Testament times, the hyssop was used in ritual cleansing.

Hyssop symbolizes humility. When David cried out his remorse and asked to be cleansed with hyssop, he acknowledged and repented from his terrible sins. David showed his humility before God, before the people in Israel, and before foreign kings.

The Old Testament is clear that God values humility. God guides the humble, gives grace to the humble, and crowns the humble with salvation. Humility is more important than both wisdom and honor (Pr 11:2, 15:33). An Israelite proverb about humility was both a warning and a reassurance: "Toward the scorners he is scornful, but to the humble he gives favor"

(Proverbs 3:34 esv). Perhaps a reason that God loved King David so much was that David was humble.

The entire concept of humility is difficult for Americans. Humility is a spirit of deference or submission. Humility is the opposite of assertiveness. Generally, being called humble is not a complement. Nonetheless, humility is a Christian virtue. Jesus was humble and described himself as a servant. In turn, Jesus calls followers to be humble.

Reflection: It's difficult to admit that we need anyone's, even God's, help. When did you last ask God to help you?

BEANS FOR A KING (2 SAMUEL CHAPTERS 15 – 18)

After years of undermining King David, Prince Absalom (David's son) went to Hebron and had himself declared King. Hebron was where David ruled Judah for seven years. Absalom had a large following of men from Israel and some from the tribe of Judah. Learning that Absalom was declared king and not knowing the extent of the rebellion, David fled Jerusalem with his household and close fighting men.

Eventually, they arrived at Mahanaim, a town about 100 miles north-northeast of Jerusalem on the east side of the Jordan River. Saul's son, Ish-Bosheth, reigned over the tribes of Israel for two years from Mahanaim. At Mahanaim, three wealthy men brought provisions to David that included meat, grains, and beans.

The bean brought to feed David's household at Mahanaim was the broad bean (*Vicia faba*). Beans are one of the oldest cultivated plants. The fruit of the bean plant is a pod that contains two-to-six fleshy beans. Harvested in about April in ancient Israel, beans were an important protein for poor Israelites. Ground beans were eaten alone or mixed with flour to make bread.

When beans were included in the provisions given to David at Mahanaim, David's benefactors were interested in providing a high protein source that would extend grain flour. Extend means "to make an offer of or to make available." David's three benefactors extended provisions to David when he was in severe need. The three men knew that they would forfeit their lives if Absalom's rebellion succeeded.

According to Hebrew proverbs, those who were kind and extended assistance to the needy are blessed and will lack nothing. In Mary's song, she averred that God's mercy extends to those who fear him from generation to generation (Lk 1:50). Individuals who revere God understand that God extends himself to us, so we will extend ourselves to others.

Reflection: How can you extend yourself to help others? Be specific.

UNIFYING THOUGHTS

Soil characteristics include color, texture, and depth. Certain soil characteristics enhance plant growth while others deter it. Some characteristics of Israel's first two kings enhanced their personal growth and the growth of the kingdom, while other characteristics hindered personal and national growth.

1. Name two personal characteristics in Saul and David that helped and two that hindered their success as kings.

2. Every man and woman is a leader in some way. Our personal characteristics can facilitate or hinder growth in our children, individuals in peer groups, or individuals who work for us. Name two of your personal characteristics which enhance and two which hinder your abilities as a leader.

3. If you wanted to enhance your positive leadership and reduce your negative leadership behaviors, list three things you could do. Did you include asking God to strengthen your abilities and behaviors? If not, consider why you didn't. Do you believe that God isn't interested in your everyday situation(s) or has more important things to do than to think about and respond to your needs?

4. Consider memorizing: "The Lord is near to all who call on him, to all who call on him in truth. He fulfills the desires of those who fear him; he hears their cry and saves them" (Ps 145:18-19 niv).

CHAPTER 7

King Solomon

§

KING SOLOMON REIGNED OVER ISRAEL 40 years (970-930 BC). He is credited with writing Song of Songs, a love story between a man and a woman, seemingly when they were young. Two plants associated with their story are the henna, which symbolized beauty, and the walnut tree, which symbolized fertility. Solomon's most famous building project was the first Temple dedicated to God. Many plants were used in Temple construction, furniture, and accessories. Three trees were the cedar, pine, and algum. Primarily, algum wood was used to make the Temple musical instruments that accompanied the Levitical choirs.

HENNA BEAUTY (SONG OF SONGS CHAPTER 1)

The book Song of Songs is a dialogue between the Beloved (a maid) and her Lover (Solomon), with minor input from Friends. According to Jewish tradition, Solomon wrote the Song in his youth prior to becoming entangled in polygamy and concubinage. This view is consistent with Song of Solomon 2:3 where the Beloved compares Solomon to other young men.

Throughout this beautiful love poem, the Beloved appeared to be Solomon's equal. Although Solomon declared his love and admiration for her, the poem seemed her love story more than his. The Beloved described almost every aspect of Solomon, i.e., his appearance, odor, and grace. Often, she compared him to plants. Solomon is like a sachet of myrrh (1:13), his fruit is sweet (2:3), his cheeks like beds of spice, and his lips like lilies (5:13). In verse 1:14, the Beloved described Solomon as a cluster of henna blossoms from the vineyards of En Gedi, meaning that he was beautiful and smelled good.

In the King James Bible henna (*Lawsonia inermis*) is called "camphire." When henna plants are about five years-old, they begin to flower and reach their peak between 6-12 years. Under ideal conditions, henna plants produce up to 25 years. In Israel, henna plants grow in the Biblical Landscape Reserve, around En Gedi, and further south in the Negev Desert if they are irrigated. Dye for hair and tattoos come from crushed leaves.

Traditionally, henna was associated with the rites of womanhood and represented seduction, happiness, and beauty. In Song of Songs, henna symbolized the beauty that the Beloved saw in Solomon. Frequently, the Bible, poets, and today's mass media associate beauty with physical attributes of women and men. The Beloved seemed to do the same; rarely did she laud Solomon's character. Jesus directed Christians to look on the inside, not on the outside, for beauty (Mt 23:27-28).

Reflection: What do you consider beautiful about your spouse? Do you tell your spouse that he/she is beautiful to you?

Love among Nut Trees (Song of Songs 6:1-12)

Solomon had expert knowledge of plants. He studied both the most majestic plants and those of little economic significance. Solomon had flower and herb/spice gardens and a grove of nut trees. In this Song of Songs entry, Solomon is the speaker although his words seem more reflective than addressed to the Beloved.

Solomon went down to the grove of nut trees to look at the new growth. Possibly, he was looking for the first signs of spring on his trees. Solomon wrote that while in the nut tree grove, "my desire set me among the royal chariots of my people" (SS 6:12 niv). The budding garden reminded Solomon of spring, a time of love. With thoughts of love, Solomon accessed a chariot to speed to the Beloved.

The nut trees in Solomon's grove were most likely walnut trees (*Juglans regia*), called the English walnut tree. During Jesus' life time, walnuts grew around the Sea of Galilee. The award-winning botanical illustrator, Winifred Walker[5] proposed that Jesus' coat was a rich brown dyed by the leaves and nuts of the walnut tree

In ancient times, the walnut symbolized fertility. Fertility is the ability to grow, develop, and produce fruit. This image of fertility is consistent with descriptions used in Song of Songs. The land's beauty and fertility were detailed, i.e., spice beds, flower gardens, groves of nut trees. At the same time, fertility in the sense of producing offspring was revealed in the love and attraction between Solomon and his Beloved.

Isaiah recorded that when God's Spirit is poured out, the desert becomes like a fertile field and the fertile field becomes like a forest. Similar to the way he makes the desert fertile, the Holy Spirit makes each of our lives fertile. The Holy Spirit promised to give us love, joy, peace, patience, kindness, goodness, faithfulness, gentleness, and self-control (Gal 5:22-23 niv). Through the action of the Holy Spirit in us, our lives can become fertile, and produce beautiful flowers, succulent fruits, and tasty walnuts.

Reflection: Is your life's garden a fertile place for the Holy Spirit, or do you need to apply some fertilizer to it? What could you use to fertilize your life?

TEMPLE CEDAR (1 KINGS CHAPTERS 5 - 7)

In the fourth year (960 BC) of his reign, Solomon started to build God's Temple on Mount Moriah. The Temple was built to worship God and to house the Ark of the Covenant and other holy furnishings. Its outside was made from stone; however, interior walls were made from gold-covered wood. The Temple was completed in seven years. Several types of wood were used, cedar, pine, algum, and olive. The Temple was decorated with plant motifs, pomegranates, lilies, palm trees, and gourds.

Solomon contracted with King Hiram of Tyre to supply cedar logs from the forests of Lebanon for the interior walls of the Temple. In exchange Solomon provided Hiram's court and servants with food. The timber arrived by rafts from Lebanon to the port city of Joppa. From Joppa, wood was transported over land to Jerusalem.

The cedar of Lebanon (*Cedrus libani*) is native to the Middle East. Cedars grow slowly. It takes centuries to produce a fully-grown cedar tree. In Israel cedar trees grow on Mount Hermon and in the Galilean and Judean mountains. Heartwood from the cedar is a warm, red, and beautifully grained.

As an expert botanist, Solomon knew cedar tree's characteristics and preferred them to trees readily available in Israel such as the sycamore and box. Cedar trees exude a gum or balsam, which gives off a scent. People love the scent. In contrast, insects dislike the smell and taste. Most insects don't attack cedar trees or wood. Wood is durable, free from knots, and easy to work.

The Hebrew word for a cedar tree comes from the root word *'âraz* meaning "to be firm."[1] Firm denotes securely or solidly fixed in place and having a structure that resists pressure. The cedar tree was firm because of its tenacious root structure, long life in nature, resistance to insect infestation, and endurance as a building material.

In the Old Testament, two themes emerged in relation to firm. The first theme was that God is firm. The second was that if God's people stood firm, he would deliver them from their enemies. At the same time, God warned Israel, "If you do not stand firm in your faith, you will not stand at all" (Isa 7:9 niv). If Israel succumbed to the life style and pressure of surrounding nations, their faith would weaken. Then, they wouldn't stand as individuals or as a nation.

Reflection: How would you describe your stand as a Christian? Do you stand firm for Jesus?

PINE IN THE TEMPLE (1 KINGS CHAPTERS 5, 6)

Construction of the Temple and Solomon's royal palace was a huge under-taking. Solomon obtained pine wood for the Temple from Lebanon. Pine trees were made into boards or planks. The Temple floor was covered with pine planks. The entrance to the Temple's main hall was two pine doors. On the doors were carved cherubim, palm trees, and open flowers. The carvings were overlaid with hammered gold.

Lebanon pine trees were most likely from old-growth forests. The wood was heartwood, taken from the center of the pine tree. Heartwood has died, hardened, and ceased to pass nutrients up the tree. It is the hardest and darkest section of the pine tree. Pine wood can be without knots (clear), have tight knots, or large knots. Tight knots add character to pine floors without appreciably weakening them. Pine heartwood ages beautifully, it darkens and takes on a soft glow. Gouges add character to pine floors. The Temple floor was a work of art that became more beautiful with use.

The most likely candidate for the Temple pine tree is the Aleppo (Syria) pine, known as the Jerusalem pine (*Pinus halepensis*). The Aleppo pine is relatively short-lived at 70-100 years; however, with care, specimens can live over 200 years. In Israel, the oldest living Aleppo pine, about 225 years-old, is in the Armenian Seminary Garden in Jerusalem. Although this pine is no longer beautiful, nor even attractive, its age makes it unique.

Pines are an emblem of nobility. Noble individuals possess excellent qualities of the mind, character, ideals, and morals. Boaz told Ruth he wanted to be her kinsman-redeemer because she was a noble woman. A woman of noble character was described as her husband's crown and was worth more than rubies (Pr 36:10).

In a brief exposition on "The Kingdom of Righteousness," Isaiah described a noble man. He wrote, "The noble man makes noble plans, and by noble deeds he stands" (Isaiah 32:8 niv). From God's perspective, nobility displays itself in actions. Jesus agreed. He said, "By their fruit you will recognize them" (Mt 7:16 niv). We recognize noble individuals (man and woman) by their actions and output.

Reflection: Think about individuals who meet Isaiah's criteria for noble. How do you feel when you are with them?

Algum Wood Musical Instruments (1 Kings 10:11-12)

Solomon wanted algum wood for the Temple; but, algum wood wasn't available in sufficient quantity in Israel. Solomon sent ships to Ophir to obtain the wood. The fleet sailed from Elath (present day Eilat), a harbor on the southern tip of Israel on the Gulf of Aqaba. Solomon contracted with King Hiram of Tyre for sailors to sail the Israelite ships.

Scholars aren't sure where Ophir was located; however, the Bible recorded that only once every three years did ships return from Ophir. The ships from Ophir carried gold, silver, ivory, apes, and baboons in addition to algum wood. Most likely, Ophir was located in India or Southeast Asia.

During Solomon's reign, more algum wood was imported than seen previously in Israel. Algum wood was used to make stairs and banisters for the Temple and royal palace. It was used extensively to make stringed instruments, i.e., harps, lyres, for Temple musicians. The musical instruments were so beautiful that they were a marvel throughout Israel.

The Bible algum and almug woods are probably the same. The algum tree is known as red sandalwood (*Pterocarpus santalinus*). Sandalwood is native to southern India and currently grows in Southeast Asia. Sandalwood is fine-grained. Although black on the surface, it polishes to a rich ruby or garnet color. Algum wood contains an antiseptic which makes it impervious to insects. At one time, algum bark and stems were made into a red dye.

Algum wood symbolized praise. The harp and lyre made from algum wood were used to praise God. Praise expresses approval and esteem. Praise is a commendation. Everything that has breath should praise the

Lord (Ps 150:6). God tells us we should praise him with our whole heart, be glad and joyful. We can use musical instruments, raise our hands, and even dance.

Reflection: New Testament Christians were exhorted to offer a sacrifice of praise to God (Heb 13:15-16). A sacrifice of praise is lips that confess Jesus' name.

Unifying Thoughts

Before serious gardeners decide which seeds to plant, they test the soil. Based on soil test results, often gardeners amend the soil with nutrients before they plant. Over years plants take nutrients from the soil; consequently, soil should be retested ever several years to make sure it remains an ideal growing environment. The soil of Solomon's life started out good. As years went by, Solomon's life-soil degenerated. He worshipped his wives' gods, overtaxed his subjects, and set his kingdom up for civil war when he died.

1. What do you think about? List the top five persons, places, things, or ideas that enter and occupy your mind.

2. How many of those five areas glorify God or are God-focused?

Solomon couldn't have a fleshly, wanton life and a spiritual mind. Because he wouldn't give up his fleshly life, Solomon's spiritual life, his communication with God, suffered.

When we accept Jesus as our Savior, all sins that we committed in the past are forgiven and wiped away by his blood. We have spiritual rebirth. It makes no sense to dwell on something that is forgiven. Yet, the Devil continues to bring up our past sins and failures to torment us.

3. Are your thoughts peaceful? Is your mind controlled by the Holy Spirit? List some specific strategies you can use to shepherd your thoughts in the directions they should go.

4. Identify what you do when the Devil bombards you with your inadequacies? Although you have your own strategies, here's an answer that works for me. When my mind is tormented, I recite the Lord's Prayer, another prayer, or Bible verses. It doesn't matter if the prayer is relevant to what I am being tormented about. By praying I replace negative thoughts with averring that God is Father; he can deliver me from all evil. Satan hates to hear us pray and acknowledge God as king. If we use this tactic time-after-time when inadequacies or thoughts of past sins arise, they will torment us less.

5. Consider memorizing: "The mind of sinful man is death, but the mind controlled by the Holy Spirit is life and peace" (Ro 8:6 niv).

CHAPTER 8

Northern Kingdom - Israel

§

Dᴜʀɪɴɢ ᴛʜᴇ ʀᴇɪɢɴ ᴏꜰ Sᴏʟᴏᴍᴏɴ's son, Rehoboam, the Israelite kingdom split into the Northern Kingdom called Israel and the Southern Kingdom called Judah (930 BC). Ten tribes formed the Northern Kingdom: Dan, Asher, Naphtali, Zebulon, Issachar, Manasseh, Gad, Reuben, Ephraim, and Simeon.

Early in their history as a separate nation, the Northern Kingdom turned to idolatry. Some of the best-known Bible prophets lived in the Northern Kingdom. Plants in these prophets' lives were the broom tree and castor bean vine. During one siege of Samaria (capital city of the Northern Kingdom), residents ate Star of Bethlehem flower bulbs.

Eʟɪᴊᴀʜ ᴀɴᴅ ᴀ Bʀᴏᴏᴍ Tʀᴇᴇ (1 Kɪɴɢs ᴄʜᴀᴘᴛᴇʀs 18, 19)

In its first 58 years as a nation, the Northern Kingdom had eight kings. When Ahab (874-853 BC) became king, he married Jezebel, daughter of Sidon's king, who worshipped Baal. Ahab built a temple to Baal and consecrated priests to serve Baal.

In an encounter with Ahab, the prophet Elijah challenged Baal's prophets. The challenge was to identify which god—Baal or God—answered his prophet(s) and ignited a sacrificial fire. Despite Baal's prophets entreating him, even cutting themselves with knives, Baal didn't set fire to their offering. In contrast, when Elijah asked God to light a sacrifice, immediately fire consumed the offering. Onlookers fell to the ground and worshiped God. Elijah commanded the people to slaughter Baal's prophets.

King Ahab reported what happened to Queen Jezebel. She sent a messenger to Elijah declaring that by that time tomorrow, she would have him killed. In terror Elijah fled Samaria and ran over 100 miles to an area in Judah south of Beersheba. Elijah came to a broom tree, sat down under it, and prayed that he would die. Disheartened, Elijah fell asleep.

An angel woke Elijah and directed him to get up and eat. Looking around, Elijah saw a cake of bread baked over broom embers and a water jar. Elijah ate and drank, then, again lay down and slept. The angel woke Elijah a second time and told him to get up, eat, and drink. Elijah ate and drank the supplied bread and water. Strengthened by the bread and water, Elijah walked to Mount Horeb in the Sinai Peninsula.

The broom tree (*Retama raetam*) that Elijah rested under is known as the white broom tree. In Israel broom trees are wide-spread. The leaf is a straight needle that drops in early autumn leaving the tree leafless most of the year. Ancient people used the broom tree as shade in the desert; coals were used for heat and baking.

The broom tree symbolized renewal. With renewal comes a restoration of vigor and a new freshness; what is faded or disintegrated is made whole. When Elijah arrived at the bloom tree, he was exhausted, depressed, and ready to die. What was to be a victory for God and Elijah turned into Elijah fleeing for his life. If anyone needed renewal, it was Elijah.

Just as God renewed Elijah using attributes of the broom tree, God renews us. Paul told Christians they could be renewed by not conforming to the patterns of this world, that is, using Sunday morning to play golf or grocery shop rather than attend worship service. *The Message* puts renewal this way, "Don't become so well adjusted to your culture that you fit into it without even thinking. Instead fix your attention on God. God will change you from the inside out" (Ro 12:2 tm).

Reflection: God, we want so badly to be renewed, to be changed from the inside out. We want to be different from the society we live in. Help us to see how we can be renewed.

Dove's Dung in Samaria (2 Kings 6:24 – 7:20)

The king of Aram, Ben-Hadad, attacked the Northern Kingdom and surrounded Samaria. Ben-Hadad's army allowed no one in or out of the city. The blockade lasted so long that a severe famine occurred. During the siege in Samaria, a quarter of a cab, equivalent to two cups, of seed pods sold for five silver shekels. To put this sum into perspective, the value of a male child one month through five years-of-age was five silver shekels (Lev 27:6).

Bibles (esv, kjv) translated seed pods as dove's dung. Dove's dung (*Ornithogalum umbellatum*) is called the star of Bethlehem plant. Possibly, the name came from seeing fields of white star of Bethlehem flowers. From a distance, the small white flowers appeared like dove's droppings. Star of Bethlehem plants grow each spring from small perennial bulbs.

The star of Bethlehem plant grows in wood-land, on mountains, and on coastal plains in Israel. In ancient Israel dove's dung was a wild flower. Botanists debated whether-or-not star of Bethlehem bulbs were edible. Some accounts described the bulb as being made into bread flour. Alternatively, chemical analysis showed that the entire plant was poisonous.

A plant specialist, James Duke,[6] harvested a few bulbs from his lawn. After vigorously boiling them without salt, he ate one. To Duke the bulb tasted like soap and had a bitter aftertaste. He added salt and found that the taste improved. Because he experienced shortness of breath following ingestion of only two bulbs, Duke concluded he would have to be near starvation to eat star of Bethlehem bulbs.

In the siege of Samaria, when the people were starving, the star of Bethlehem bulb was food. The bulb was valued and valuable. When individuals want something, they value it. Being and acting godly are important attributes for Christians. Paul reminded Timothy that physical training is of some value, but training for godliness has more value. When we emulate Jesus' actions and obey God's word, we train ourselves and God trains us to be godly. Being godly is valuable both for our present life and most assuredly for our life after death.

Reflection: What is valuable to you? Not sure? Look at what you do, how you spend your time, and importantly how you spend your money. That will tell you what you value.

THE PARABLE OF THE THISTLE (2 CHRONICLES CHAPTER 25)

King Jehoash ruled the Northern Kingdom for 16 years (798-782 BC). He did evil in God's eyes; yet, he won a significant battle over King Amaziah of Judah. The incident between Kings Jehoash and Amaziah began when Amaziah challenged Jehoash to meet him in battle. King Jehoash sent a parable back to Amaziah that contained a riddle and a warning.

The message was: "A thistle in Lebanon sent a message to a cedar in Lebanon, 'Give your daughter to my son in marriage.' Then, a wild beast in Lebanon came along and trampled the thistle underfoot" (2 Ch 25:18 niv). King Jehoash warned King Amaziah that he was haughty and proud; but he was asking for trouble if he persisted in challenging Jehoash.

The interpretation of Jehoash's parable was that he and the Israelites were the majestic cedar of Lebanon while Amaziah and Judah was an insignificant thistle. If Judah declared war on them, Israel would trample Judah under their feet. Despite King Jehoash's warning, King Amaziah moved his army against Israel. Jehoash's army won the battle against Judah and subsequently plundered the Jerusalem Temple and the palace treasury.

In the Bible, about 20 different words are associated with some type of prickly or thorny plant. In King Jehoash's parable, the Hebrew word for thistle is *choâch¹* (*hoah*). When Jehoash named Amaziah a thistle, possibly he was thinking of the spotted golden thistle (*Scolymus maculatus*). The spotted golden thistle grows throughout Israel except along the Mediterranean seashore. Often the spotted golden thistle grows in uncultivated lands, i.e., abandoned fields, ditches, along paths and trails.

King Jehoash's comparison of King Amaziah to a thistle was an insult. His words were insolent and contemptuous of the King of Judah. Clearly, Jehoash wasn't trying to appease Amaziah's anger against him; just the opposite. The insult was designed to ferment dissension between the two kingdoms.

Christians view insults differently than Kings Jehoash and Amaziah. Jesus told people of his day and by extension Christians in the twenty-first century to feel blessed when persecutors insult them and lie about them because these same types of people insulted the prophets. Jesus' zeal for God caused men to insult him. On one occasion Pharisees even said that Jesus worked for Satan (Mt 12:24)!

In our Home Group, I shared that sometimes I am unsure if I am being persecuted for righteousness sake or if the persecution is the result of some offensive behavior in me. King David must have had similar feelings. He asked God to "See if there is any offensive way in me" (Ps 139:24 niv). When King David asked God to see if there was any offensive way in him, he asked God to search him, know his anxious thoughts, and lead him in everlasting ways.

Reflection: How is David's prayer a strategy to identify and deal with offensive ways in ourselves?

Death of Jonah's Vine (Jonah chapter 4)

Jonah's theme is that God's divine mercy is applied without favoritism to Jew and Gentile. At God's direction, Jonah went to Nineveh and proclaimed, "Forty more days and Nineveh will be overturned" (Jonah 3:4 niv). The Ninevites believed Jonah and repented in sackcloth and ashes. Because the Ninevites repented, God had compassion and didn't destroy Nineveh.

The Ninevites were relieved over God's decision; however, Jonah was angry. He thought that he wasted his time going to Nineveh. Perhaps, Jonah worried he was no longer a credible prophet because God didn't follow through on his announced plan to destroy Nineveh. Jonah went to a spot east of Nineveh and built a small shelter. He sat under the shelter and waited to see what would happen. Jonah had no confidence that the Ninevites would continue their reformed ways.

God stimulated a vine to grow over Jonah to screen him from the sun. Jonah was happy for the shade. At dawn the next day, God made a worm chew the vine so it withered. Then, God caused a scorching east wind and the sun to shine on Jonah's head. Jonah grew faint and told God that he was better off dead.

God asked Jonah if he had a right to be angry about the vine dying. Jonah's retort was a resounding "I do and I am angry enough to die" (Jnh 4:9 niv). God responded that Jonah was concerned about a vine that he neither caused to grow nor tended. How much more should God be concerned about Nineveh, a city of 120,000 people who didn't know right from wrong?

Jonah's vine was the castor bean plant (*Ricinus comminus*). Castor bean plants grow wild in Israel. Although the fruit is referred to as a bean, it is a seed. The "oil" of castor oil is largely from the seed and is an effective laxative. Ricin, a deadly poison, can be made from seeds.

In Jonah's story, the castor bean plant symbolized compassion. Compassion is awareness of another person's distress, along with a desire to alleviate it. God had compassion on the Ninevites; however, Jonah had no compassion for the Ninevites, even after they repented. Possibly, Jonah's lack of compassion resulted from viewing God as belonging to the Israelites. Jonah didn't fully understand that God was the God of the universe, not of one nation.

Throughout the book of Jonah, God leads Jonah to a new understanding of himself. God was never angry with the sulky Jonah. Instead, God gave patient explanations to Jonah using Jonah's feelings for the vine to parallel God's compassion for the Ninevites.

Reflection: Where or what is Nineveh to you? Are there groups of people or nations for which you have no compassion and spend no or little time praying for?

Innocent and Chaste as a Lily (Hosea chapter 14)

A minor prophet, Hosea lived in the final disastrous days of the Northern Kingdom when six kings reigned within 25 years. Hosea came from the north; he knew every pride and perversion of its people. Although Hosea emphasized God's love, mercy, and forgiveness, he averred that Israel's disloyalty to God and their idol worship were spiritual adultery.

Hosea implored the Northern Kingdom to repent so that God could heal their waywardness. God wanted to turn his anger from them! God said that if Israel repented, he would be like dew falling on the land and Israel would blossom like a beautiful lily. From earliest time dew symbolized God's blessing on Israel (Dt 33:13).

The Hebrew word for lily is *shôshân* (*shôwshannâh*), which means a "beautiful flower."[1] The lily is the most mentioned flower in the Bible. Ancient Israelites believed that the lily was dear to the heart of God. Over time the lily became known as the Star of David, which appears on the modern Israeli flag.

Hosea's lily (*Lilium candidum*) is called the Madonna lily because it appears in pictures with the Virgin Mary. In Latin, *Lilium* means "shining or pure white." Lilies originated in the Middle East and Greece. In Israel, wild lilies grow in Mediterranean wood-land and shrub-lands, i.e., Carmel and Upper Galilee. Cultivated lilies grow from bulbs throughout Israel. In the Christian church, the lily symbolizes resurrection and is used to decorate churches at Easter.

In Hosea chapter 14, the lily symbolized chastity and innocence. Chastity means abstaining from unlawful sexual intercourse. If Israel stopped worshiping idols, they could be chaste before God. They would no longer commit spiritual adultery. Innocence is freedom from guilt or sin by being unacquainted with evil. If Israel repented and returned to God, then God would restore their innocence. Their previous spiritual adultery wouldn't have occurred. God was willing to make the degenerate Northern Kingdom chaste and innocent, similar to a young man or woman who never had sex or even thought about sex.

Through Jesus, God invites each of us to become chaste and innocent, no matter our sins, crimes, or idols. Chastity and innocence occurs when we have a new birth by accepting Jesus as Savior. We can maintain our chastity and innocence by confessing ongoing sins to God (1Jn 1:9).

The more I think about confessing daily sins to God, the more I believe that the activity is for me rather than for God. By confessing my sins to God, I rid myself of all things that stand between him and me. When I sin, God doesn't move away from me; but I move away from God. Confession restores my closeness to God.

Reflection: Do you feel innocent and chaste before God? Are you ready to give up spiritual adultery in your life in return to God-given innocence and chastity?

Unifying Thoughts

Fertilizers are added to soil to supply nutrients essential for plant growth. After Israel separated from Judah, God didn't cease to fertilize Israel. Some of the most outstanding Bible prophets—Elijah, Elisha, and Hosea—were sent to beg Israel to repent from their sins. The Israelites knew God from family stories, the Book of Law, and from prophets; however, they deliberately chose to ignore God. They preferred to wither and fade rather than to be beautiful flowers in God's garden.

1. How do Christians move from flourishing in God's garden to being willful sinners? Complete the three-part table below:

How movement from God occurred?	What could have prevented movement from God?	How to stop or short-circuit deliberate, sinful behavior?

2. Are we our brother's or sister's keeper in relation to spiritual matters, or is it best to not judge others and let them be responsible to their own actions and conscious? Why or why not?

3. How are you a fertilizer in Jesus' soil to your family, on your job, and among non-Christian friends and acquaintances?

4. Consider memorizing: "For anyone who knows the good he ought to do and doesn't do it, sins" (Jas 4:17 niv). Does this verse cause you to feel a little uncomfortable? It sure does me.

CHAPTER 9
Southern Kingdom - Judah

§

Two TRIBES, JUDAH AND BENJAMIN, formed the Southern Kingdom (930-586 BC); however, at times Benjamin aligned itself with the Northern Kingdom. Often the Southern Kingdom was simply called Judah because Judah was so much larger than Benjamin and because Judah was the more stable member of the Southern Kingdom.

The nation of Judah is remembered for its mix of evil and excellent kings, many of whom had direct connections to plants. For example, Isaiah warned King Ahaz that because of his actions, the land of Judah would become thorn-infested. Zephaniah announced God's approaching judgment on Moab and Ammon using the burning nettle. Jeremiah associated the balm of Gilead plant with healing.

JOEL'S SHRIVELED APRICOT TREE (JOEL CHAPTER I)

The prophet Joel recorded the effect of a locust scourge on Judah's agriculture. Plants were destroyed and the harvest ruined. Field crops were decimated; grains and vines eaten. Plants not destroyed by locusts dried up and new seeds shriveled beneath clods of dry soil. Because there were no pastures or fodder, livestock suffered. Fig trees were stripped of fruit, leaves, stems, and bark. Other trees, pomegranate, palm, and apple, dried up.

The year of the locust invasion was a horrible year for Judah. Because Judah's agriculture was destroyed, people suffered from insufficient food and nutrients. Imported food was scarce and costly. Even in subsequent years, the nation's food supply was reduced. Seeds didn't germinate during the locust year; consequently, no seeds were available to plant the next growing season. Farmers purchased seeds from other nations at inflated prices. Heavily damaged vines and trees took years to recover, that is, to grow new branches and produce fruit.

Israeli botanists believe Joel's apple tree was in reality an apricot tree (*Prunus armeniaca*). The apricot tree is native to northern China. Probably, it was introduced into Mesopotamia and Israel about 2500 BC. In *Correspondences of the Bible: The Plants*, Worcester[2] suggested that sweet fruit trees such as the apricot symbolized pleasant encouragement for good.

When used in the Bible, encouragement means "to give help, to lift a person's confidence, or to strengthen their purpose." In the Old Testament, several people and groups needed encouragement. God told Moses to encourage or inspire Joshua because Joshua would lead the Israelites into the Promised Land. Israelite solders strengthened comrades with words of encouragement before and during battles. The righteous were entreated to encourage and give aid to the afflicted, oppressed, fatherless, and widows. Certainly, when locust devastated Judah, the people needed encouragement.

Paul identified that Scriptures were intended to encourage Christians so they could have hope. Repeatedly, Paul wrote that he was encouraged when he learned that Christian churches were thriving. Paul rejoiced that his imprisonment encouraged his brothers to speak the word of God courageously and fearlessly

My husband visits an 84-year-old man at the Virginia Veteran's Care Center and I visit a 100-year-old woman in a retirement home. When we started these weekly visits, we had the idea that we would minister to them and encourage them. Probably, we quietly patted ourselves on the back for our outreach efforts. Now, we know that we are the ones who receive encouragement from visits with these elders. We offer them nothing that we don't receive back in double measure.

Reflection: Is encouragement part of your intentional Christian effort? How can you be an encourager to your enemies?

KING BURNS TEMPLE INCENSE (2 CHRONICLES CHAPTER 26)

Uzziah became king of Judah when his father was murdered. He reigned 52 years. Initially, Uzziah did right in God's eyes and God gave him success. With success, Uzziah became proud and unfaithful to God. He entered the Temple and began to burn incense on the Altar of Incense. According to Mosaic Law, only consecrated priests could burn Temple incense. The chief priest, Azariah, and 80 courageous priests confronted Uzziah and demanded that he leave the Temple sanctuary.

When King Uzziah began to rage against the priests, leprosy broke out on his body. From that time until his death about 10 years later, Uzziah lived in a house separate from the palace. His son, Jotham, ruled Judah. Uzziah was buried in a field near his ancestors; however, he wasn't buried in the royal tombs because of the leprosy.

The composition of Tabernacle incense was stacte (gum resin), onycha, galbanum, and pure frankincense. In this chapter, stacte represents the plant used in Temple incense. Although arguments abound about the origins of stacte, credible botanists believe it came from the styrax tree (*Styrax officinalis*). The tree originated in Eastern Mediterranean countries. In Israel, styrax trees grow on Mount Herman and in central mountains and valleys.

The Hebrew word for stacte comes from *nâtaph*, which means "to ooze in the sense of distill gradually or to fall in drops."[1] The figurative meaning of *nâtaph* is "to speak by inspiration," i. e., prophesy. God's breathed out words into the words of the prophets and the Holy Scriptures. As styrax exuded gum resin (stacte), God exuded and exudes his message into the world.

As we talk about Bible passages, we often say "as David said in Psalm 51" or "as Paul wrote." We need to remember that Bible authors wrote under the influence of the Holy Spirit. The words in the Bible aren't words of ascribed authors, i.e., David, Jonah, Paul. Words in the Bible are God's message to humanity.

In Sunday worship, our pastor identified that a Christian essential is to believe that the Bible as the inspired Word of God. He pointed out that some individuals—even those who identify themselves as Christians—believe that parts of the Bible are God-inspired, while other parts aren't. This latter perspective is bewildering, i.e., how am I to know which parts are and aren't inspired? Also, the inspired versus uninspired Bible portions could be a moving target, similar to psychological and perceptual morality.

God wanted to teach and fellowship with us so much that he breathed his words into a book. He created the Bible, a world-wide best seller. The Bible is the "go to" book for Christian devotions. Although reading Bible commentaries and studies (even this one) are good for spiritual growth, nothing can take the place of reading the Bible, God's word given directly to us.

Reflection: How intentional are you about reading the Holy Bible?

Becoming Trash (Isaiah chapter 7)

Isaiah (740-681 BC) was the first of three major prophets; he wrote the book Isaiah. He ministered during the reigns of Jotham, Ahaz, Hezekiah, and early in the reign of Manasseh. The Bible identified both Jotham and Hezekiah as kings who walked with God. In contrast, Kings Ahaz and Manasseh were two of the wickedest kings to rule Judah.

From the start of his 16-year reign, Ahaz rejected God. He burnt incense to idols and offered sacrifices to them on hill tops and under trees. Ahaz sacrificed his son to a false god. When the Arameans and the Northern Kingdom (Israel) joined to attack Jerusalem, God sent Isaiah to reassure Ahaz that Jerusalem wouldn't be razed. At the meeting Isaiah directed Ahaz to ask for a sign of God's intent to protect Jerusalem. Ahaz refused, saying that he wouldn't test God.

Isaiah replied that Ahaz's refusal to ask for a sign tested God's patience! He prophesied that in the next 12-13 years both Aram and Israel would be laid waste; and God would bring devastation on Judah. Where there were a thousand vines worth a thousand shekels, the land would be covered with briers and thorns. When men went among them, they would carry bows and arrows for protection. Cattle and sheep would run loose in the brier and thorn-infested land.

The thorn plant that was part of Isaiah's prophecy is the buckthorn (*Rhamnus lycioides*). In Israel, buckthorn grows primarily on the sides of Mount Hermon and in wood-lands and shrub-lands. It produces a berry that is poisonous to humans, but can be eaten by birds with no ill-effect.

In Isaiah 7:23-25, the Hebrew word for thorn is *shayith*, which means "scrub and trash."[1] Trash is debris from plant materials, something worth little or nothing; often trash is discarded. Trash is an excellent symbol for what was going to happen in Judah because King Ahaz led the people to reject God. Because Ahaz treated God and the Temple like trash, Judah would become the trash that King Ahaz and Judah's citizens claimed for themselves. Formerly fertile fields would become trash-infested as punishment for Judah's sin.

God's judgment isn't confined to the Old Testament. In the twenty-first century God's judgment falls on people who treat him and his laws as worthless (Ro 1:28-32). If individuals want to be trash, God allows them to be that way. Sadly, God gives them over to a reprobate mind as he did most people in Judah.

Reflection: Do you treat any portion of God's word as something that can be disregarded or thrown away? Do you pick and choose which of God's commandments to obey?

Burning Nettle Prophecy (Zephaniah 2:8-11)

Zephaniah lived in Jerusalem and ministered during the early years of King Josiah's reign. Zephaniah is three spell-binding chapters that announced God's pending judgment on Judah and on nations living in the region. Zephaniah's prophecy which included the nettle plant was against Moab and Ammon. Both the Moabites and Ammonites were offspring of Lot's incestuous unions with his two daughters. From the time Israel attempted to pass through Moab on the way to the Promised Land, Moab was Israel's enemy.

Zephaniah began his prophecy against Moab and Ammon by writing that God heard their insults, taunts, and threats against Judah. God was aware of the pride of the Moabites and Ammonites. In retaliation for their behavior, Moab would become like Sodom and Ammon like Gomorrah. Both would become places of nettles and salt pits, a wasteland forever.

God's declaration that their countries would become like Sodom and Gomorrah should have alarmed the Moabites and Ammonites. Lot and his daughters once lived in Sodom. Ancestral history would have included tales of God raining burning sulfur on the two cities. The outcome was destruction of cities, people, and vegetation on the Sodom and Gomorrah plain.

Zephaniah's nettle (*Urtica urens*) is the burning nettle. It is a beautiful-looking green plant that when touched causes itching and burning in almost everyone. In Zephaniah's prophecy, the nettle symbolized fire and burning. Fire results in light, flame, and heat. Burning means to destroy by fire. Sodom and Gomorrah were burnt to the ground.

In comparison to Sodom and Gomorrah, the behavior of Moab and Ammon didn't seem that extreme—their sin was taunting and insulting Judah and threatening to occupy Judah's land. To understand the extent of Moab and Ammon's taunts, remember Ezekiel's words: Ammon rejoiced maliciously when God's Temple was desecrated (Eze 25:3). When Moab saw Judah vulnerable and Jerusalem sacked, they believed God was beaten. The Moabites didn't recognize that Judah and God were separate. God was more than a local deity. He was God of the universe.

Today, many individuals don't believe in the one true God. Some believe alternative religions, while others believe in no God. Hopefully, with God's help we can grab or clutch some of these individuals from the fire of disbelief. If not, their names won't appear in the Book of Life (Rev 20:14-15). Their destiny is the Lake of Fire.

Reflection: Should we be politically correct and encourage everyone to have their own personal beliefs? Do Christians have any responsibility for non-Christians' final destinies?

JEREMIAH AND BALM OF GILEAD (JEREMIAH CHAPTERS 8, 46, 51)

Jeremiah was a Levite, possibly from the priestly family of Abiather (David's reign) and Eli. His home town, Anata, was three miles northeast of Jerusalem. His writings were filled with examples from nature and agriculture. Jeremiah was in Jerusalem when the Babylonians conquered (586 BC) it. Although most of the elders and leaders of Jerusalem were killed or deported to Babylon, Jeremiah remained free.

Jeremiah mentioned the "balm of Gilead" plant three times and in association with three different countries. First, he lamented Judah's destruction and exile. Jeremiah asked, "Is there no balm in Gilead? Is there no physician there? Why then is there no healing for the wound of my people?" (Jer 8:22 niv). Second, Jeremiah prophesied against Egypt. Jeremiah advised Egypt to go to Gilead and get balm; however, Jeremiah knew that the balm wouldn't heal Egypt. Third, Jeremiah suggested Babylon obtain balm to heal itself. At the same time, Jeremiah wrote that Babylon couldn't be healed because her sins were too great. Although God used Babylon to exact judgment against Judah, in God's time Babylon was to be destroyed for the country's extreme brutality.

Jeremiah's balm of Gilead (*Balanites aegyptiaca*) is called Jericho balsam and desert date. In Israel, it grows in the Mediterranean wood-lands and in deserts. Jericho vendors sell tins labelled "balm of Gilead" to tourists. The "balm" looked like a salve; however, I'm not sure what it is made from.

Fredrik Hasselquist, an eighteenth-century pioneer in the study of Holy Land plants, provided detailed information on the balm of Gilead plant and its uses.[7] According to Hasselquist, the balm is a yellow, light-reflecting gum. Plant leaf, stems, and roots produced the glutinous, tenacious gum. The gum sticks to the fingers and can be drawn into long threads; consequently, Turkish surgeons used the gum to hold the edges of wounds together. Using balm of Gilead gum to treat wounds is consistent with Jeremiah's question of where was the balm of Gilead to heal the wounds of his people.

Medically, balms give pain relief. They are a healing or soothing ointment, salve, or cream. Figuratively, balms calm and comfort; they provide solace and consolation. Jeremiah asked for pain relief for Judah, which included relief for people's physical wounds and comfort for their spirits. Remember the old hymn:

> There is a balm in Gilead
> To make the wounded whole.
> There is a balm in Gilead
> To heal the sin-sick soul.

Reflection: What is a sin-sick soul? Was your soul ever sick? What is the best way to deal with a sin-sick soul?

Unifying Thoughts

As I read over Chapter 9, the gardener part of me saw Judah resembling insects. Insects can be beneficial, but they can also be harmful to mankind. Beneficial insects pollinate fruits and vegetables, provide food for birds, and produce honey and silk. On the negative side, annually, insects destroy millions of dollars of crops, trees, and household items. Similarly, some of Judah's kings benefited their country but others harmed it. Some kings led citizens into a deeper relationship with God, while others led them into sin and idolatry.

1. Think about your church. In one column list three activities done by members that are beneficial to the body of believers and reflect God's precepts.

Beneficial activities	Harmful or irrelevant activities

2. Now, list three activities that could be or are harmful to the body of believers. These activities can also be unrelated to Jesus or the mission of the church to spread Jesus' good news.

3. Go back and put an X in front of each activity that you participate in. Are any of them harmful, detrimental or irrelevant to Christianity? Just because an activity is held in the church doesn't make it beneficial to the spread of Jesus' kingdom.

4. How does the following verse from Joel apply to your life? Consider memorizing it: "I will repay you for the years the locust have eaten …. my great army that I sent among you" (Joel 2:25 niv).

5. Do you have any wasted years in your life? Name a few wasted periods of time. What have you learned from the wasted years? Are you aware and grateful that God is going to redeem them? No, God won't give you a chance to re-live them; but, he will free you from the distress and harm of those years. He will repair and restore your wasted years.

CHAPTER 10
Captivity and Restoration

§

PLANTS IN THE LIVES OF Jews during the Babylonian captivity and the restoration periods are the topics of Chapter 10. The time frame is about 160 years (605-444 BC), from the time the first captive was deported from Jerusalem to the return of Nehemiah to Jerusalem. Plants that demonstrated the captivity grew in Babylon; they were the millet and the willow tree.

After the Persians conquered the Babylonians, they allowed Jews to return to Jerusalem and rebuild God's Temple and the city walls of Jerusalem. The first group of Jews returned in 537 BC. Trees in the restoration period were the citron and myrtle. The lives of Jews who remained in the Persian Empire improved under Persian rulers. Esther, a young Jewish woman, became the wife of King Ahasuerus (Xerxes) (486-465 BC) and queen of Persia. The royal palace in Susa had curtains made from cotton.

EZEKIEL'S PARABLE OF FAMINE BREAD (EZEKIEL CHAPTER 4)

Ezekiel was a prophet and priest who lived in Babylon. He was exiled to Babylon before the destruction of Jerusalem. God called Ezekiel to proclaim a message of judgment against Judah. Much of the judgment focused on Jerusalem, the political, religious, and social hub of Judah.

In Babylon, Ezekiel foretold the siege of Jerusalem in a series of action parables. In one action parable, Ezekiel represented God's judgment through a famine. God told Ezekiel to bake a cake of bread to eat each day. The bread was made from wheat, barley, beans, lentils, millet, and spelt. Taken together the grains and legume weighed about eight ounces. With the bread Ezekiel drank about 22 ounces of water. The amount of bread and water was famine rations.

The meaning of Ezekiel's parable was that God would cut off the bread and water supply to Jerusalem. Inhabitants would waste away because of their sin. The famine would be so severe that when Jerusalemites looked at each other, they would be appalled by their emaciated appearance.

The Biblical millet (*Panicum miliaceum*) was used in Mesopotamia by 3000 BC. Supposedly, a head of millet produces about 1,000 seeds, thus the name *miliaceum*. Millet is the smallest of all cereal grains. No early traces of millet were found in Israel.

In Ezekiel, millet symbolized famine which led to starvation and death. Almost every famine documented in the Promised Land was God's punishment for Israel's sins, i.e., rejection of God and worship of idols. God told Ezekiel that 1/3 of Jerusalem's population would die of pestilence or famine, 1/3 would be killed by the sword, and 1/3 would be scattered to the winds (exiled).

Most of us living in the West never experienced famine which leads to starvation; however, Jesus warned followers that near the end of the ages, famines will occur over the entire earth. Famine in ancient Jerusalem resulted from its people's sins. Similarly, near the end of the ages, world-wide famine will be a consequence of sin. Most likely, famine will occur in the United States and in other westernized countries.

Reflection: Famine can be mental as well as physical. Do you know anyone who is starving for God and his Word? Consider specific ways you can help them.

Harps Hung on Willow Trees (Psalm 137)

On August 14, 586 BC, the Babylonians set fire to the Temple, royal palace, and every important building in Jerusalem. The walls of Jerusalem were broken down. Many people in Jerusalem were taken as captives to Babylon where they were treated as slaves. Psalm 137 remembered the Babylonian captivity and provided insight into the captives' lives in Babylon.

The first stanza (verses 1-3) showed the captives were wretched. At times, they could do nothing but sit and weep for their lost freedom and land. Verse 2 recorded that the Jewish captives hung their harps, used to accompany songs to God, on willow trees. Probably, the men didn't technically hang their valued musical instruments on willow tree branches. More likely, they set them aside or as we say today, "put them on a back burner," having no heart to play or sing.

The focus of Stanza 2 (verses 4-6) is repentance. The captives take curses on themselves if they forget Jerusalem, i.e., may their tongues cling to the roof of their mouth if they don't remember and consider Jerusalem their highest joy. Stanza 3 (verses 7-9) is a petition for God to punish the Edomites and the Babylonians. The Edomites encouraged the Babylonian soldiers' brutality when they destroyed Jerusalem.

The Babylonian willow (*Salix babylonica*) is called the weeping willow. An ancient person interpreted the downward growth pattern of branches and leaves as sadness, hence the name "weeping." Probably, returning Jewish exiles brought the weeping willow tree to Judea from Babylon. The Babylonian willow grows in Israeli wood-lands and on the Sharon Plain.

Depression and weeping could be associated with the Babylonian weeping willow tree because they describe the feelings of the Jewish captives in Ps 137:1-3; however, "repentance" is the better symbol. Repentance means "turning from sin and amending one's life." Repentance implies sorrow, regret, and contrition for previous sinful behavior. The captive Jewish men repented; therefore, they couldn't sing God's songs in a land of idolaters. They saw moral impropriety in mixing God's songs with the things of the world.

In April 1948 immediately before Israel declared its independence, the Jewish section of Jerusalem was practically under siege.[8] Food supplies were almost exhausted. Then, news came that a convoy of food was coming from Tel Aviv. Jews in Jerusalem reported that they will never forget the sight of the first truck in the convoy. Written on the front bumper of the blue Ford were the words "If I ever forget you, O Jerusalem…" The Jews of 1948 remembered the repentance of their fathers 2,500 years earlier.

Reflection: Like the Jews in the food convoy from Tel Aviv to Jerusalem, we can remember our own repentance. Oh, what a glorious day!

Goodly Fruit in Festival of Booths (Ezra 3:1-6)

King Cyrus of Persia conquered Babylon in 539 BC. He decreed that the Jewish people could return to Jerusalem and re-build the Temple to their God. In 537 BC, about 50,000 Jews along with their live-stock arrived in Jerusalem. Several months later the Jews assembled in Jerusalem. They rebuilt the Altar of God and sacrificed both morning and evening burnt offerings. Then, the returned exiles celebrated the Feast of Tabernacles.

The Feast of Tabernacles was called the Festival of Sukkoth (booths). The Festival was both a reminder of the 40 years the Israelites wandered in the wilderness, living in temporary shelters, and a celebration of the fall harvest. It lasted seven days. During all, or some portion, of the seven days, Jews lived in temporary shelters (booths) which they built to mirror their ancestors' sojourn in the Sinai wilderness.

The four sacred plants of the Festival of Tabernacles were the palm tree, willow tree, myrtle tree, and citron fruit. A palm leaf, two willow stems, and three myrtle stems were bound together and held in the right hand. Citron fruit was in the left hand. Jews recited a blessing and waved the four species in six directions (east, south, west, north, up, and down) to symbolize that God was everywhere.

The citron (*Citrus medica*) is called goodly fruit. The original goodly fruit of Leviticus was probably a cedar or pine cone; however, by the restoration period the citron was the accepted goodly fruit. The fruit is green initially. As it ripens, it turns yellow. Goodly fruit resembles a lemon; but, the outside skin is rippled rather than smooth.

God promised to give the returned exiles a hope and a future (Jer 29:11). When the returned Jews celebrated Sukkoth with the citron, they demonstrated hope. The archaic or ancient definition of hope is "desire, accompanied by expectation that the desire will be fulfilled." The Festival of Tabernacles was a time for the returned exiles to come together as a community, to praise God for his care, celebrate the fall harvest, and hope—expectantly believe—in a prosperous future.

Reflection: For twenty-first century Christians, hope comes from trusting Jesus. Hope is aided by understanding that the current earth isn't our home. Indeed, Christians live as strangers in this world.

Vision among the Myrtle Trees (Zechariah 1:1-17)

The prophet Zechariah was born in Babylon. He traveled to Judah with the first group of returning Jewish exiles. Zechariah received eight visions in one night. In the first vision Zechariah saw a man riding a red horse.

The man stood in a ravine among myrtle trees. Behind the man were other horsemen. The man explained to Zechariah that the horsemen were the riders that God sent throughout the earth. The returned riders reported that the world was at peace.

Hearing the rider's reports, the Angel of the Lord (generally thought to be the pre-incarnate Christ) asked God how long he was going to withhold mercy from Jerusalem. God reassured the Angel that he was jealous for Jerusalem and Zion and angry with nations who punished the Jews. They went too far in their brutality against Judah. God's plan was to punish the offending nations and turn to Jerusalem with comfort and mercy. God promised that Judah's towns would again overflow with prosperity.

At one time, wild myrtle trees (*Myrtus communis*) were common throughout Israel; however, today most are cultivated and ornamental. Occasionally, wild trees are seen in the Upper Galilee and Golan areas. The myrtle is one of the four blessed plants used in the Jewish Festival of Tabernacles (Sukkoth). To fill the requirement for Sukkoth, three myrtle leaves must grow from one point on the myrtle stem.

Zechariah's vision of horsemen, angels, and God among myrtle trees reinforced God's promise that the returned exiles would be prosperous. Prosperity means a person or a group "thrives or flourishes," especially in financial or economic terms. For the Jews of Zechariah's time to prosper, God required that they repent, serve the Lord, and rebuild the temple.

The challenge for many Christians is that we see people, who have no regard for God or his laws, get ahead (prosper) in the workplace and in society. The great prophet Jeremiah asked God "why does the way of the wicked prosper? Why do the faithless live at ease?" (Jer 12:1 niv). God's response to Jeremiah and to all of us is that evil individuals will sow wheat but reap thorns. They will wear themselves out, but gain nothing. God was telling Jeremiah that even if a man was rich on earth, if he lacked eternal life, he had nothing.

Reflection: Does God reward godly people with prosperity? Does God reward ungodly people with failure and loss? Where is God in the prosperity equation?

Hiding behind a Cotton Curtain (Book of Esther)

Esther is the story of a beautiful Jewish girl who became the wife of Ahasuerus (Xerxes), king of Persia (486-465 BC). The story begins with Ahasuerus giving an elaborate banquet in the palace's enclosed garden. The garden had white cotton curtains and violet hangings fastened to silver rings on marble pillars. During the banquet, Ahasuerus commanded that Queen Vashti come before banqueters to display her beauty. Vashti refused. Subsequently, Ahasuerus divorced Vashti and Esther became queen.

Later, the King's advisor, Haman, convinced Ahasuerus that Jews were enemies of the Persian Empire. Ahasuerus ordered that all Jews be slaughtered on the same day. Esther's uncle, Mordechai asked Esther to intervene with King Ahasuerus on the Jew's behalf. After prayer and fasting, Esther told the king that she was a Jew.

King Ahasuerus was stunned. He didn't realize that in ordering the death of all Jews, he ordered the death of Queen Esther. Angrily, Ahasuerus commanded his servants to hang Haman who initiated the plan to kill Jews in the Persian Empire. Because Ahasuerus couldn't undo his previous decree, he made another one which allowed the Jews to destroy any armed forces that might attack them.

The white cotton (*Gossypium herbaceum*) used in the palace garden curtains was known as Levant cotton and Arabian cotton. Cotton plants were domesticated in India about 3000 BC and used in Mesopotamia as early as 1000 BC. Ahasuerus ruled lands from India to Ethiopia. Finding cotton curtains in his palace is reasonable. The cotton flower often starts out pink, then, turns yellow, before it forms a boll which contains cotton fibers.

Curtains had several meanings to include (a) a hanging screen that can be drawn back, (b) a device that conceals or acts as a barrier, and (c) the time that a theatrical performance begins. In the Susa palace cotton curtains reflected all three meanings. The curtains were tied back by cords when weather was pleasant. They were a hanging screen which protected garden visitors during inclement weather or to obscure the sun's rays (barrier). Finally, the cotton-curtained plaza was the stage on which the first act of the drama of Esther began, a drama that included Esther saving the Jews in the Persian Empire.

When Jesus died, the Jerusalem Temple curtain or Veil tore from top to bottom. Jesus' death opened a way for Christian believers to have direct access to God. There is no longer a curtain that obscures God from his children. Through the blood of Jesus, Christians confidently approach the Throne of Grace and stand before God.

Reflection: The God of the universe is your beloved Father, Abba. No one loves you more than God loves you.

UNIFYING THOUGHTS

Often, God referred to the Israelites as vines or trees which he tended. When fruit-bearing trees and vines are pruned, they produce higher quality fruit. Pruning includes cutting away diseased, weakened, and dead wood. Captivity and restoration demonstrated how God cut diseased wood from Judah so that profitable fruit could develop.

1. Identify three activities that are diseased, dead, or weak wood in your life which need to be pruned. Ask God to help you to rid yourself of each activity.

2. Did you notice when you read Chapter 10 how God vindicated his people; i.e., God used the Babylonians to punish Judah for its sins. Yet, God punished Babylon for their excessive brutality. How has God vindicated your life and activities?

3. Are you ever brutal or less loving than you could be with your spouse, children, or in a work situation? If so, how can you change your behavior? It is so easy to see brutality in others; but, ignore our own brutality. Pray for a loving, less brutal heart. Pray that the fruit of the Holy Spirit will increase in your life and your ego will decrease.

4. Consider memorizing: "Not by might nor by power, but by my Spirit, says the Lord Almighty" (Zec 4:6 niv).

CHAPTER 11
Jesus' Birth and Early Ministry

§

CHAPTER 11 BEGINS NEW TESTAMENT time and focuses on Jesus' birth and Galilean ministry. At Jesus' birth, wise men from far off Persia (Iran) offered valuable plant products to the newborn child. When Jesus communicated—whether in sermon, parable, or action—he provided directions for followers to live by.

In the Sermon on the Mount, Jesus illustrated godly truths with plants, i.e., flowers growing in a field. Later, Jesus contrasted John the Baptist with a reed because of John's unbending convictions. One of Christ's parables focused on an enemy sowing weeds in a wheat field. Another used the mustard seed to describe small beginnings and faith. Clearly, Jesus understood plants and how they grew. He used many of them in his parables and other teachings.

BABY GIFTS (MATTHEW 2:1-18)

When Jesus was born in Bethlehem, Judea, wise men came from the east to worship him. The visiting wise men followed a star from Persia to Judea. They believed that the star signaled the birth of a Jewish king. Initially, the wise men went to Jerusalem. There, they learned that Messiah was to be born in Bethlehem. They left Jerusalem and followed the star to that small town. The star stopped moving over the house where Joseph, Mary, and Jesus lived. Seeing Jesus, the wise men fell on their knees and worshipped Jesus. They gave Jesus gifts of gold, frankincense, and myrrh. Frankincense and myrrh were made from plants.

After the wise men left Bethlehem, God ordered Joseph to take Mary and Jesus to Egypt to escape being killed by King Herod. The family stayed in Egypt until God told Joseph it was safe to return to Judea. Probably, Joseph used the wise men's gifts to subsidize the family's trip to Egypt and their lives there.

Both the frankincense tree (*Boswellia sacra*) and its resin are called frankincense. Frankincense doesn't grow in Israel except where cultivated as an example of a Bible plant. The best frankincense looks like a yellow-white crystal; reddish frankincense is an inferior quality. Frankincense is described as smelling like aromatic pine plus flowers.

Frankincense was used in Jewish religious ceremonies from the time of the Tabernacle. So complete is the link between frankincense and religious occasions that frankincense is known as the "odor of sanctity" and associated with sainthood. Sanctity implies a holy life and character, a life worthy of religious respect.

Saints were recognized in both the Old and New Testaments. Psalmists averred that God delights in the saints and preserves them; they lack nothing. God guards the feet of the saints (1Sa 2:9). When individuals acknowledge Jesus as Lord, they become saints. The Holy Spirit intercedes on behalf of the saints so their prayers and actions are consistent with God's will (Ro 8:27). Loving words from God are,

"Precious in the sight of the Lord is the death of his saints" (Ps 116:15 niv).

Reflection: Have you ever thought of yourself as a saint? How could thinking of yourselves as a saint impact your behavior?

Flowers among Field Grass (Matthew 6:25-34)

Jesus gave the Sermon on the Mount in Galilee. Jesus stood at the bottom of a hill, while listeners sat in the grass at higher elevations, similar to an amphitheater. The Sermon on the Mount was Jesus' inaugural address. His words are the standard for Christian life. Jesus told listeners that lilies adorned grass and challenged them to apply the analogy of beautiful flowers adorning simple field grass to their lives. He asked them: If God cared enough about simple (not so pretty, ordinary) field grass to clothe it with beauty, wouldn't God clothe and care for his people?

When Jesus used the example of lilies, he didn't mean the true lily identified by Hosea. Jesus was referring to a flower that grew wild and abundant in the fields, was colorful, and known to people in the crowd. The lily of the field was probably the crown anemone (*Anemone coronaria*), sometimes called a windflower. It grows in every part of Israel. Petals can be white, pink, purple, blue, or red. Red petals are more resistant to harsh growing conditions; they abound in steppes and desserts. Anemones can grow in full sun or in mixed sun-shade.

The crown anemone has been associated with the Trinity, sorrow, and death; however, when Jesus referred to it in the Sermon on the Mount, he spoke of "worry." Three times in the Matthew 6:25-34 passage, Jesus told the people to not worry. He identified that individuals need not worry about their life, including what they wear, eat, or drink. Worrying doesn't change the need for these items.

Worry does nothing but disturb an individual's peace of mind as the same thoughts intrude, minute after minute, hour after hour, and day after day. Worry keeps us awake at night and interferes with much-needed sleep. Worry makes us irritable and often causes us to say unkind words.

An alternative to worrying is to take our concerns to God. We are assured that when we take requests to God, he gives peace back to us (Php 4:6-7). Plus, when we take our worries to God, he guards our heart and minds so we are no longer consumed with useless thoughts.

Reflection: How does worry change a situation? What are you saying to God when you worry?

John and a Reed (Luke 7:18-35)

At the beginning of Jesus' public ministry, John baptized Jesus. Soon afterward, King Herod Antipas imprisoned John because John openly disapproved of Herod's marriage to Herodias, originally the wife of Herod's brother (Mt 14:3-5). While in prison, John sent two disciples to ask Jesus if he was the Messiah. Jesus didn't give John's disciples a direct "Yes" or "No" answer. Instead Jesus told the disciples to go back to John and report what they saw and heard, i.e., the blind received their sight, the lame walked, and lepers were cured.

After John's disciples left, Jesus asked the crowd what they expected when they went to the desert to see John. Did they expect John would be a reed swaying in the wind, a man dressed in fine clothes, or a prophet? When Jesus asked the crowd if they expected to see a swaying reed, he contrasted a swaying reed with the firmness of John's convictions and message. John's message didn't depend on his audience. He had the same message for tax collectors, religious leaders, and rulers: repent, for the kingdom of heaven is at hand! John wasn't politically correct. He never altered his message to accommodate an audience. Unlike a reed that swayed and bent in the wind, John didn't bend under the harshest winds of adversity

The reed that Jesus referred to when talking about John was the giant reed or the Cypress cane (*Arundo donax*). Reed colonies are located along banks of running water, in flood plains of streams, and on dry river banks far from permanent water. Pilgrims to Israel can see reeds growing along the Jordan River. In ancient Israel, giant reeds were made into brooms and woven into mats and wall screens.

In the vignette about John the Baptist and the reed, the symbolism is conviction. A conviction is a "firmly held belief" that something is true, real, and certain. John lived his convictions. John stayed on message (repent) and on task (baptize). Today, the world has an even stronger voice than John to convict us of sin. The Holy Spirit convicts individuals of original sin, their need to repent, accept Jesus as Savior, and be baptized. Likewise, the Holy Spirit convicts Christians of ongoing sins they commit daily. When we listen, the Holy Spirit tells us which parts of our lives are righteous and which are sinful. Then, we can make judgments about aspects to change.

Reflection: Would family and friends identify you as a firm or straight reed for Jesus or do you bend and sway with societal pressures?

WEEDS IN A WHEAT FIELD (MATTHEW 13:24-30)

Jesus was seated by the Lake of Galilee when he told the parable about weeds in a wheat field. A farmer planted good wheat seeds in his field. Good seeds were without weeds and contaminants. At night the farmer's enemy sowed weeds (tares, darnel) among the wheat. When the wheat sprouted and formed heads, so did the weeds which intermingled with the wheat.

A servant asked the farmer if he should pull out the weeds. The owner said "No" and explained that if the weeds were removed, wheat roots could be damaged. The farmer directed servants to let both wheat and weeds grow together until harvest time. Then, they could go through the fields, pull out the weeds and burn them. Harvested wheat would be secured in the owner's barn.

Here is the parable's interpretation. The field is the world and the farmer is God. Initially, God sowed good seed, meaning individuals who followed him. Satan sowed weeds into the world, that is, individuals who rejected or were indifferent to God. The servants were God's angels. Harvest represented the second coming of Jesus. At this time, angels will send God-rejecters to the lake of fire and gather God-followers into God storehouse (heaven).

In the parable of the weeds, the weed (*Lolium temulentum*) is darnel, also called poison ryegrass. Darnel is distributed widely in Israel. It infests wheat fields and other cultivated land. Initially, darnel plants are green; they look a lot like wheat. As summer progresses, darnel turns black. Darnel's black color is a good way to differentiate it from wheat which is creamy brown.

The enemy who sowed weeds among the good wheat was malicious. He wanted to destroy the good wheat that the farmer grew. The farmer's enemy was spiteful and mean. An Old Testament proverb focused on maliciousness: "A malicious man disguises himself with his lips; but, in his heart, he harbors deceit. Though his speech is charming, do not believe him" (Pr 26:24-25 niv). This proverb admonishes us not to be fooled by a malicious man's words.

The New Testament contains instruction about maliciousness. Jesus told disciples that if a person's heart and thoughts are unclean, he will spew forth all kinds of unclean words, such as slander, malice, and deceit (Mk 7:20-23). In a way, it is good that our hearts and words are so closely aligned. Hearing our malicious words is a clue that there is something wrong with our hearts.

Reflection: Think back over your week. Were any of your words malicious, spiteful, or deceitful? What can you do to change some of your thoughts and words?

LITTLE FAITH, BIG RESULTS (MATTHEW 13:31-32, 17:19-20, LUKE 17:5-6)

The first time Jesus talked about the mustard seed was in a parable about the kingdom of heaven. Jesus told the crowd that the kingdom of heaven is like a mustard seed, one of the smallest of all seeds. Yet, when planted in a field, the mustard seed becomes a large garden plant. Birds come and perch on branches. The meaning of the parable is that although Jesus' kingdom will begin small, it will expand throughout the entire world. People from all nations will take refuge in it.

When Jesus mentioned the mustard tree *(Salvadora persica)*, likely he referred to the toothbrush tree that grows up to 20 feet-tall, rather than the much shorter black mustard plant *(Brassica nigra)* in United State gardens. In Israel, the mustard tree grows in the Judean Desert, Dead Sea Valley (around En Gedi), and in the southern Israel deserts.

From ancient times, the mustard seed was associated with faith. Faith is a firm belief in something, or someone, for which there is no proof. Although Christians in the twenty-first century don't physically see Jesus, we believe in him and his father, God, and the Holy Spirit who comes to live in each of us when we confess Jesus as Savior.

Through the work of the Holy Spirit, a small religious group known, initially. as "The Way," grew into a world-wide religion that has lasted for 2,000 years. The disciples of The Way had faith in God and shared their faith with other individuals, who shared their faith with others, who shared their faith with others. Today, we have a world-wide communion of Christian believers.

Refection: How do you define faith? Does faith ease the circumstances of your life or make it harder?

UNIFYING THOUGHTS

When I looked back over the plant symbolism in Chapter 11, I noticed that all the concepts were positive. Plants don't have a soul or a spirit; but, they give us joy, regenerate, and are even trustworthy. We can be like beautifully cultivated plants because God is our gardener. God wants us to grow according to his plan and receive all the bounty that he can shower on us.

1. Reflect on what God has given to you. In the first column of the table, list the beautiful things, items, relationships, etc., that God gave to you.

God gave me	What I want yet from God	How to partner with God?

2. In the second column, identify what you would like God to give you in addition to what you have. Be thoughtful, careful, and prayerful about this column. The nice thing about plants is that if you decide you don't like an annual or even a perennial, you can

pull it up and put another plant in its place. It isn't quite the same with aspects of our lives.

3. In the third column, think about how you could partner with God to obtain what you don't have, but want. Think and pray about your answer. Once a prayer is answered, often we have to live with the answer. Have you asked for things that are consistent with Holy Scripture?

4. How can you better acknowledge and celebrate the gifts God has given you; for example, a spouse, a child, a sibling, a wonderful church, or a soft chair for your devotions? God gives us big gifts and small gifts; let's not forget the small ones.

5. Consider memorizing: "Lord, you have assigned me my portion and my cup; you have made my lot secure. The boundary lines have fallen for me in pleasant places; surely I have a delightful inheritance" (Ps 16:5-6 niv).

CHAPTER 12

Jesus in Perea and Judea

§

AFTER LEAVING GALILEE, JESUS TRAVELED southward into Perea and Judea.
Perea is the land east of the Jordan River, often called Trans-Jordan.
Christ continued to use plants to illustrate physical and spiritual reali-
ties of life, both in the current time and at the end of the ages. Plants
in Jesus' ministry in Judea and Perea include an herb, a pod, two trees,
and a perfume. In the five episodes in Chapter 12, Jesus demonstrated
his frustration over the wrong thinking and behavior of Pharisees while
celebrating the lives of a tax collector and a woman who put their trust in
him. The perfect substitute for sins, Christ wanted individuals to turn to
him without delay.

TITHING ON MINT (LUKE 11:37-44)

One day a Pharisee invited Jesus to eat at his house. Jesus entered the
house and reclined at the table. The Pharisee was surprised that Jesus
didn't wash his hands before the meal; most foods were eaten with the
hands. After a full day of outside activity and in contact with many individuals, Jesus' hands were dirty. Although not a Mosaic Law, many Jews
advocated hand washing before meals.

Knowing his host's thoughts, Jesus remarked that Pharisees clean the
outside of dishware, while they disregard the inside which is full of greed

and wickedness. Jesus went on to say that Pharisees tithe on mint, rue, and garden herbs, but neglect justice and love of God.

Mosaic Law required that Jews tithe. Tithing meant Jews gave 10% of their income and/or crops to the Lord. Most herbs were grown in family gardens and consumed by the family; however, when herbs were sold, sellers were required to tithe on income from the sale. Because only small amounts of herbs were sold and selling costs were low, the tithe on herbs was miniscule.

Noteworthy, Jesus didn't tell the Pharisees that tithing on herb sales was wrong. Just the opposite, Jesus reinforced the need for God's people to tithe, even on small amounts of profit. At the same time, Jesus instructed the Pharisees that loving God and seeking justice were the greater good.

The mint (*Mentha longifolia*) that grew in the Holy Land was often called wild mint or Sinai mint. Wild mint smells and tastes like peppermint. If a mint plant is propagated for a specific aroma or taste, pieces of the original root should be replanted. In Israel, mint grows in Galilee and the central mountains and valleys. In the southern Negev Desert, kibbutzim grow mint in irrigated gardens.

The Greek word for mint is derived from *hēdista*, meaning "gladly" or "with pleasure."[1] King David associated righteous behavior with gladness and joy (Ps 68:3). Supposedly, the Pharisees were righteous. They should have been glad and joyful; yet, I found no place in the Bible where Pharisees were described that way. Is it possible that David was wrong? There is no association between righteous living and gladness or joy? Or was there something wrong with the righteousness of the Pharisees?

William MacDonald[8] wrote that Pharisees weren't happy or joyful because they were externalists. While punctilious about small details of ceremonial law, i.e., hand washing, they neglected the greater commandments to love God and neighbors. Pharisees emphasized their own subordinate rules and regulations while ignoring those of God.

Reflection: Would you describe yourself as glad and happy? If your answer is "No," what changes are you going to make in your life?

The Prodigal and the Pods (Luke 15:11-32)

Jesus told the parable of the lost, or prodigal, son in response to criticism for eating with sinners. This parable was one of three parables that made the point that God searches for the lost, whether a lost sheep, coin, or person. The parable of the prodigal son goes like this:

A father had two sons. The younger asked his father for his inheritance. After receiving it, he went to another country and squandered the money. Then, a famine occurred in that country. The youth hired himself to a citizen, who sent him to feed pigs. He was so hungry that he wanted to eat the pods fed to the pigs. Eventually, the young man came to his senses and decided to return home. He planned to tell his father that he didn't deserve to be called a son; he would gladly work as a hired hand.

While the prodigal son was a long way off, his father saw him. The father ran to his son, hugged, and kissed him. The son confessed that he was unworthy to be called son. Before he could ask his father to treat him like a hired hand, the father ordered servants to bring new clothes and a ring for his son's finger. The father ordered a feast to celebrate the lost son's return.

The pods that the prodigal son longed to eat were carob pods, fruit of the carob (*Ceratonia siliqua*) tree. Carob trees are called locust tree and the carob fruit named St. John's bread after John the Baptist. Carob trees were only found in Israel after the restoration; possibly, they were brought from Babylon by exiles who returned to Judea. Carob trees grow throughout Israel. Initially green, pods turn brown before harvest. They taste like cocoa.

The genus name of the carob tree, *Ceratonia*, comes from the Greek word *kĕras* (κέρας), meaning "horn," the shape of the carob pod.[1] Carob pod flour is often called "poor man's" flour. Bread from carob pods is associated with humility. Symbolisms such as horn and humility make sense in the lost son parable; however, so does substitute. Substitute means "to exchange, or switch, or replace with something else." In this parable, substitute is what the younger son did. He substituted his life as a valued son for a life of shameful living and feeding pigs. He replaced eating the best foods with yearning to eat carob pods. He planned to ask his father to substitute his role as son for that of hired hand.

From a Kingdom perspective, Jesus substituted his perfection for our sin. Because of his substitution, we can run to the Father with joy. We don't have to make deals with God, i.e., "I've sinned unbelievable, God; just let me come into heaven as a servant." Because of Jesus' substitution, God walks out to meet us with open arms. What in the world are we to do with love this big, so underserved?

Reflection: Would the prodigal son have been saved if he never returned home and asked his father's forgiveness?

MOVING A MULBERRY TREE (LUKE 17:1-6)

In a teaching about a mulberry tree, Jesus outlined three responsibilities for his disciples. One was to never lead a person into sin. A second was to rebuke a brother if he sins. The third was to forgive a brother if he repents of sin and asks for forgiveness.

After hearing Jesus' words, the disciples were over-whelmed with the extent of their responsibilities as his followers. In desperation, they cried out to Jesus, "Increase our faith!" (Lk17:5 niv). Jesus gave them a simple response: If you have faith the size of a mustard seed, you can tell a mulberry tree to be uprooted and transplanted into the sea. With sufficient faith, the mulberry tree will obey.

The mulberry tree (*Morus nigra*) is known as the sycamine tree. Although there are red and white mulberry trees, the black mulberry grows in Israel. In modern Israel, mulberry trees grow wild and are domesticated. Initially, fruit are green, change to red, and when ripe are black and filled with large amounts of water.

The mulberry tree is called the "wisest of all trees" because it waits to bud until all danger of frost is past. The genus name, *Morus*, comes from the Latin word *mora* which means "delay." Delay means "to postpone or to put off to a later time."

When the disciples asked Jesus to increase their faith, his response was that they only needed a small amount of faith to accomplish great acts, that is, move a mulberry tree. Wisely, Jesus delayed requiring them to have a large amount of faith in him. Rather, he met them where they were in their walk with him and knowledge of him. Later, when Jesus went to the cross, died, and rose, he required the disciples to have faith in him "now," without delay. By that time the disciples knew more about Jesus' character, who he was, and what he taught. They were ready—with no further delay—to believe fully in Jesus as Messiah.

Reflection: At some point, we must to stop delaying our decision to have deep, abiding faith in God. We must make the decision to fully trust him.

Zacchaeus in a Sycamore Tree (Luke 19:1-10)

Zacchaeus was a Jew who worked as the chief tax collector for the Romans in Jericho. Many tax collectors including Zacchaeus became rich from overtaxing and defrauding individuals in their tax districts. Jews named tax collectors "sinners" along with adulterers, prostitutes, and robbers.

Physically, Zacchaeus was a short man. Because he wanted to see Jesus, Zacchaeus climbed into a sycamore tree by the side of the road where Jesus was walking. To Zacchaeus' surprise, Jesus stopped under the sycamore tree where he was perched. Jesus looked up and started talking to Zacchaeus. What Jesus said was shocking not only to Zacchaeus, but to the crowd who was with Jesus. Jesus told Zacchaeus to come down from the tree because he was going to stay at Zacchaeus' house that day. Zacchaeus climbed down from the sycamore tree and welcomed Jesus into his home.

Jesus' visit brought about a radical change in Zacchaeus' life. Following their time together, Zacchaeus vowed that he would give 50% of his possessions to the poor. To individuals he cheated, Zacchaeus would pay back fourfold. Zacchaeus' promised restitution was more than the Hebrew law demanded (Lev 6:4-5). Where once, Zacchaeus was controlled by greed, he was now controlled by love. J e s u s' response to Zacchaeus' conversion was to declare that salvation came to Zacchaeus' house.

The sycamore tree (*Ficus sycomorus*) that Zacchaeus climbed was known commonly as the sycamore fig. Sycamore fig trees live up to 1,000 years; however, because sycamore trees don't have annual rings, it is hard to ascertain exact age. The sycamore fig is about one-half inch in diameter and has the consistency of a peanut. In a tour of Jericho several years ago, the guide showed us the sycamore tree that Zacchaeus (supposedly) climbed to see Jesus. The tree trunk and limbs were gnarled and old; however, the tree wasn't old enough to be the actual tree Zacchaeus climbed 2,000 years ago. Possibly, the current sycamore tree is a cherished offspring of the tree climbed by Zacchaeus.

In the Bible story of Jesus and Zacchaeus, the sycamore tree symbolized regeneration. Regeneration refers to someone who is spiritually reborn. Zacchaeus had spiritual rebirth through his discussion with Jesus; the result was a regenerated heart. Zacchaeus' new heart caused him to make restitution to people he cheated in his home town of Jericho.

After regeneration or spiritual rebirth, often it is easier to start over in a new place; but, Zacchaeus didn't leave town. It must have been difficult for Zacchaeus to daily see men and women whom he cheated. It must have been beyond difficult for Zacchaeus to admit that he was a cheat and to make restitution for money he defrauded his neighbors.

Reflection: Have you ever thought about making restitution for sins you committed that hurt others? How can you move from thinking to doing?

JESUS ANOINTED WITH NARD (JOHN 12:1-11)

All four gospels recounted a story of a woman anointing Jesus with perfume. John identified that Jesus was anointed at Lazarus' home in Bethany, Judea six days before Passover and prior to his triumphal entry into Jerusalem. As Jesus reclined at a table during a meal, Mary entered the room with an alabaster jar of very expensive perfume made of pure nard. She broke the jar seal and poured the perfume on Jesus' feet. Mary wiped Jesus' feet with her hair.

Some banquet guests were indignant. They asked why the perfume wasn't sold and the money given to the poor. The value of the nard was worth more than a year's wages in Jesus' time. Aware of their indignation, Jesus told the mutterers to leave the woman alone. He explained that what she did was beautiful. Jesus predicted that wherever the gospel is preached, the story of the woman anointing him would be told in memory of her act. The disciples only later realized that Mary anointed Jesus for burial.

The New Testament nard (*Nardostachys grandiflora*) was often called spikenard. Spikenard is made from the rhizomes (roots) of the plan. Spikenard doesn't grow naturally in Israel. In the Roman Empire, the most valuable perfume was nardinum, made from spikenard. Probably, spikenard was an ingredient in Temple incense in Jesus' time. The photograph is the American spikenard (*Aralia racemosa*).

The Greek word for spikenard is *pistikŏs* which means trustworthy in the sense of "genuine or unadulterated."[1] In this story the nard used to anoint Jesus was pure or unadulterated. Mary's love for Jesus was so overwhelming that she entered a room where a meal was served to men only. She humbled herself to anoint Jesus' feet. Mary saw Jesus as trustworthy. She didn't expect him to reject her offering or expel her from the room. Jesus is always trustworthy when individuals seek him. He never rejects those who seek him regardless of their previous sins.

Paul described Jesus' character and emphasized Jesus' trustworthiness. Here's what Paul (2 Ti 2:13 niv) wrote: "If we are faithless, he (Jesus) will remain faithful for he cannot disown himself." Even when we are not faithful to Jesus, he remains faithful to us. Like the woman with nard who trusted that Jesus wouldn't reject her, you, too, can trust Jesus.

Reflection: How do you demonstrate that you trust God?

Unifying Thoughts

Most of the plants Jesus dealt with in Chapter 12 were perennials. Perennials regrow year-after-year. Often the top of the plant dies back in winter; however, roots persist underground. In our Christian walk, many of us resemble perennials. At times, we reduce our outward Christian activity, but our root-stock is good. We are firmly grounded in our faith and spiritual life.

1. How many hours a week do you spend in church and church-related activities? List these activities and calculate (roughly) the total number of hours.

2. About how many hours a week do you spend alone with God? What do you do in this time?

3. Compare your answers to question 1 and 2. Do you ever substitute your church activities for personal time with God?

Developing a Christian walk takes personal time with Jesus; time when we read our Bibles, pray, and meditate. It's great if we have time for church organizational activities; but, these activities can't substitute for, or take precedence over, our personal time with God.

4. Consider memorizing: "The Lord will guide you always; he will satisfy your needs in a sun-scorched land and will strengthen your frame. You will be like a well-watered garden, like a spring whose water never fails" (Isa 58:11 niv).

CHAPTER 13
Events in Holy Week

§

HOLY WEEK BEGINS ON THE first day of the week, the day that Christians call Palm Sunday, and ends the following Saturday, which is the Jewish Sabbath. Jesus encountered over 15 plants during Holy Week; five are included in Chapter 13. These plants point to Jesus as lion and healer. They depict the shame and cruelty of mankind. Supposedly, Judas hung himself on the beautiful redbud tree.

By tradition the cross on which Jesus was crucified was made from a dogwood tree; however, the dogwood tree isn't native to Israel. In New Testament times, it didn't grow in Israel. Generally, Israeli botanists haven't speculated on the tree used for Jesus' crucifixion.

LION'S TOOTH IN THE LAST SUPPER (LUKE 22:7-23)

Christians call the Passover meal Jesus celebrated with his apostles the Last Supper. The meal was held in a large, furnished room in a man's home. Probably, the room was on the second floor, an upper room. The upper room was south of the Temple, near the Gihon Spring. A path led from the home, through the Kidron Valley, to the Mount of Olives and garden of Gethsemane. The date for the Passover meal in 33 AD was Thursday, April 22.

In the Last Supper, the central food was a roasted one year-old unblemished male lamb. This lamb pointed to Jesus, the Lamb of God, who was sacrificed for our sins. Another food was bitter herbs that symbolized the Israelites bitter life in Egypt. The type of bitter herb wasn't specified. In New Testament Israel, chicory, lettuce, and dandelion were typical bitter herbs used in Passover.

The dandelion (*Taraxacum officinale*) illustrates bitter herbs used in the Last Supper. Dandelions grow from early spring into late autumn. In Israel, supposedly the dandelion grows from the extreme north at Mount Hermon to the southern Negev Desert. The word dandelion comes from the French phrase *"dent de lion"*, which means "lion's tooth" because of the jagged shape of leaves. Dandelion, the bane of home owners and farmers, hardly seems to warrant such a grand French name.

The Bible compared both Jesus and Satan to a lion. Jesus is the Lion of the tribe of Judah, a Messianic title. Peter warned that Satan prowls like a roaring lion looking for someone to devour (1 Pe 5:8). Satan isn't an imaginary fellow with horns and tail. He isn't a cartoon character. The devil (Satan) is pure evil.

There are several ways that Christians can confound Satan. We can

- live self-controlled, rather than out-of-control, lives (1 Pe 1:13)
- be alert to Satan's seductive tactics
- resist Satan and stand firm in our faith in Christ (Jas 4:7)
- pray that we won't be led into temptation, but delivered from evil one.

Christians are assured that they will never be tempted beyond what they can bear (1 Co 10:13). With every temptation that comes our way, God has already provided a way for us to escape it.

Reflection: Will the dandelion ever be a simple weed again?

Suicide on a Redbud Tree (Matthew 26:1-27:10)

Judas was one of the 12 apostles. He was called Judas, son of Simon, and Judas Iscariot. Iscariot means "man from Kerioth." Kerioth was a town located in the northern Negev. Possibly, Judas Iscariot was the only non-Galilean apostle. Judas kept the community purse for Jesus' followers. According to the apostle John, Judas was a thief.

Judas went to the chief priests to negotiate payment for betraying Jesus. The priests were delighted and offered him 30 silver coins. Judas agreed on the amount and the chief priests paid him immediately. From that time onward, Judas looked for an opportunity to betray Jesus that wouldn't cause a riot among his followers.

Following the Last Supper, Jesus and disciples went to the Garden of Gethsemane to pray. Knowing that Jesus spent his nights in Gethsemane, Judas guided an attachment of soldiers, officials, and Pharisees to Jesus. Judas told them that the man he kissed would be Jesus. Approaching Jesus, Judas said, "Greetings, Rabbi" and kissed him. Christ was arrested and taken to the high priest, Caiaphas. During the night, the priests and elders questioned Jesus. By early Friday morning, they decided Jesus should die. They put him in shackles and handed Jesus over to Pilate, the Roman governor. The Jewish leaders demanded that Pilate crucify Jesus. When Judas saw that Jesus was condemned, he was filled with remorse. He tried to return the 30 silver coins to the chief priests and elders, saying that he betrayed Jesus' innocent blood. Callously, the Temple priests responded, "What is that that to us? That's your responsibility" (Mt 27:4 niv). Judas threw the money on the Temple floor, left the Temple, and hung himself.

For centuries, the red bud tree (*Cercis siliquastrum*) has been associated with Judas Iscariot's death. According to legend, when Judas hanged himself on the tree, the tree's white flowers turned red. In Israel, the redbud tree grows in the northern and central regions. The Biblical Landscape Reserve and Jerusalem Botanical Garden both name the redbud tree the "Judas' tree."

The symbolism of the redbud tree is shame and remorse. Shame means feeling disgraced, guilty, or inferior. The redbud tree's shame wasn't because Judas hanged himself, but because Judas used it as the vehicle for his death. Matthew wrote that Judas was seized with remorse after betraying Jesus' innocent blood. Remorse includes gnawing distress from a sense of guilt. Probably, Judas felt shame, remorse, and guilt.

The difference between the redbud tree and Judas was that the redbud tree changed its flowers from a pristine, beautiful white to crimson to atone. Judas' sin was much greater than that of the redbud tree; yet, Judas made no effort to atone for what he did. Instead, Judas committed suicide to escape his feelings.

Reflection: Are you bogged down by shame and remorse over a past act? Jesus desires and accepts repentant hearts. He uses sinful men and women, even ones who denied him at one time in their lives.

DELIBERATE CRUELTY (MARK 15:15-20; JOHN 19:1-16)

After Pilate ordered Jesus to be crucified, he turned Jesus over to his soldiers. The Roman soldiers took Jesus to the Praetorium, the soldier's quarters. There, the soldiers flogged Jesus. To mock his claim that he was a king, they put a purple robe on Jesus. Purple was the symbol of royalty. Instead of a jewel-encrusted gold crown or the traditional Roman crown of flowers, the soldiers put a crown of thorns on Jesus' head. The crown's thorns dug into Jesus scalp adding more pain to his whipped and tortured body.

The soldiers called out to Jesus mockingly, "Hail, king of the Jews." (Mt 27:29 niv). Repeatedly, they struck Jesus on the head and face with a staff. The soldiers spit on Jesus in parody of the traditional kiss given to Roman rulers. After the soldiers had sufficient "fun" torturing him, they put Jesus' clothes back on him. They led Jesus through the streets of Jerusalem to the crucifixion site. The crown of thorns wasn't removed from Jesus' head; it went with Jesus to the cross.

The crown of thorns was made from the Jerusalem thorn (*Paliurus spina-christi*) plant called Christ's thorn. Plant stems and twigs are flexible and hairless. They have a pair of unequal length, hard, sharp, spines (thorns). The longer of the two spines can be one inch. Stem and twig flexibility made the Jerusalem thorn ideal to interlace into a thorn crown.

Suggested symbols of the Jerusalem thorn tree are grief, tribulation, and sin. Although these are valid symbols, an alternative symbol of the Roman soldiers' treatment of Jesus is deliberate cruelty. A cruel act is one devoid of human feelings when grief, pain, and injury are inflicted. Jesus had been condemned to death and flogged. It was deliberate cruelty that caused the soldiers to ridicule him or to place a braided thorn crown on his head.

Reflection: Think about times when your behavior was cruel, either deliberately or by simple neglect of something you could have done. How can you be less cruel?

Jesus Refused a Narcotic (Matthew 27:32-40)

Golgotha was the site of Jesus' crucifixion. The Roman soldiers offered Jesus a drink of wine mixed with gall. When Roman soldiers felt pity for a prisoner before crucifixion, they added gall to wine and offered it to prisoners. After tasting the drink, Jesus refused it.

The soldiers pounded nails into Jesus' hands and feet to attach him to the cross. Then, they positioned the cross upright into a hole in the ground. Jesus hung from the cross, held in place by the nails in his hands and feet. Jesus was crucified at about 9:00 in the morning.

By Roman law, the reason a man was crucified had to be written at the top of the cross, i.e., murderer, thief, insurrectionist. The reason for this law was so that all who passed by would know the reason for the cruel method of death. The inscription on the top of Jesus' cross was, "This is Jesus, The King of the Jews" (Mt 27:37 niv).

The gall in the wine offered to Jesus was distilled from the opium poppy (*Papaver somniferum*) flower. Archeological evidence showed that the opium poppy was cultivated for at least 4,000 years. It grew in the northern and central regions of Israel. In the United States, it is illegal for home gardeners to grow opium poppies.

Opium is a narcotic, sedative, and hallucinogen. Gall would have reduced the pain Jesus felt from the torture and crucifixion. With opium, Jesus would have felt sleepy. The poppy's hallucinogenic effect would have reduced Jesus' contact with reality. Despite advantages to drinking gall, Jesus refused it. He was determined to experience both the physical and mental pain associated with redeeming mankind. As Jesus hung on the cross, he was in excruciating pain and fully alert.

On the cross Jesus continued to care about people in this world. He reached out to a thief who was crucified beside him. When the thief repented, Jesus assured him that today he would be with Jesus in paradise. From the cross Jesus ensured a home for his widowed mother with the apostle John.

Jesus knew the sign over his head said, "King of the Jews." Even while enduring unbelievable pain on the cross, Jesus knew he was the King of the Jews. His grief over the lack of insight of the Jewish leaders added to his pain. Today, Jesus continues to feel pain for his unrepentant brothers and sisters. I believe Jesus still asks, "What else can I do for you? What more can I do to draw you to me, to cause you to repent?"

Reflection: Would it have made a difference in the redemption process if Jesus was sedated on the cross and his pain blocked?

ALOE-WRAPPED BODY (MARK 15:42-46, JOHN 19:38-42)

Mosaic Law required that Jews bury a dead man's body the same day he died so the land wouldn't be desecrated by an unburied body. Jesus died about 3:00 p.m. on a Friday afternoon. Friday was the Day of Preparation for the Jewish Sabbath, which began about 6:00 p.m. On the Sabbath, Jews couldn't do any work to include burying a dead body. Jesus' followers had a three-hour window of time to prepare his body and bury him before the start of the Sabbath celebration.

Joseph of Arimathea, a prominent member of the Jewish council, believed that Jesus was the Messiah. Boldly, Joseph went to Pilate and asked for Jesus' body. After confirming that Jesus was dead, Pilate released Jesus' body to Joseph. Along with Nicodemus, Joseph took Jesus' body off the cross. The two men wrapped the body in linen strips and 75 pounds of mixed aloe and myrrh. After laying Jesus wrapped body in a garden tomb, a large stone was rolled against the entrance.

New Testament Jews believed that spices retarded decay and covered the smell of a decaying body. Aloes don't have an aroma. Likely, the aloes were used to "set" or "fix" the odor of myrrh. The aloe of the New Testament was the common aloe (*Aloe barbadensis,* formerly named *aloe vera*). Aloes may be the oldest known medicinal plant. Normally, aloe plants bloom in April and May in Israel; however, bloom times vary with external temperatures. Flowers grow on a central spike and are often yellow. A watery liquid or gel in the aloe leaf is used for topical healing, i.e., burns, cuts, scrapes. Older, larger aloe leaves contain the most gel.

Traditionally, aloes were associated with healing; however, when Jesus' body was wrapped with aloes, they weren't there to heal him. Jesus was dead. He couldn't be healed by aloes or medication from the most renowned physician. Instead, in Jesus' burial the aloes symbolized healing for mankind. The purpose of Jesus death was so that mankind, you and I, could be healed.

After Jesus' resurrection, some individuals in Judea and the Roman Empire accepted healing from Jesus. Other individuals weren't willing to be healed. Some couldn't comprehend that a man would die for their sins. Others simply didn't believe that they were all that bad; why would someone need to die for their few sins? For still others, it was easier to continue their same religious observances, i.e., make an animal sacrifice or give a little money to a synagogue or church, than to accept a new way of thinking. The rationale and rationalizations that individuals used 2,000 years ago for not accepting healing from Jesus are the same ones that individuals use today.

Reflection: Ultimately, spiritual health is more important than physical health. How's your spiritual health?

UNIFYING THOUGHTS

No matter how favorable the soil, climate, or temperature, plants can't live without water. Water is a valuable, but finite, resource. Jesus, a spring of living water, is infinite—endless, immeasurable, and limitless. God gave Jesus to the world and took Jesus from the world, but not until Jesus completed his work in the world.

1. Have you ever had the occasion to rejoice in suffering? What caused the suffering? What caused the rejoicing?

2. Imagine living life daily, knowing that you are going to be flogged, spit on, and crucified.

3. Reflect/discuss: As Jesus suffered, faithful Christians can expect to suffer for the sake of Jesus, the Christ.

4. Consider memorizing: "He who did not spare his own son, but gave him up for us all—how will he not also, along with him, graciously give us all things?" (Ro 8:32 niv).

CHAPTER 14
Early Church Letters

§

THE EARLY CHURCH LETTERS ENCOMPASSED 23 books of the New Testament; 13 (57%) were written by St. Paul. Generally, Paul didn't illustrate his teachings using plants. Both James and Peter used flowers of the field to discuss the brevity and perishable nature of man's life.

Among early church letter writers, St. John identified the largest number of plants. He predicted that near the end-times, a blazing star with the name of a plant (wormwood) would fall to earth. John prophesied both the collapse of the Roman Empire and the end of the ages. When the world's commerce and economic systems failed, commodities that would no longer be available included several plant products, i.e., cinnamon and myrrh.

WILD FLOWERS AND THE RICH (JAMES 1:10-11)

Many early Christians viewed riches as a reason for pride. Riches bought comfort, prestige, and worldly goods. In contrast, James wrote that riches were a reason for humility. James' rationale was that the rich man will pass away like a wild flower. With the heat of a scorching sun, the wild flower withers, its blossoms fall, and its beauty fades. Similarly, a rich man will fade away as he goes about his business.

James contrasted the behavior of the financially poor and rich. The poor are rich in faith; however, the rich exhibited few signs of faith.

Instead they exploited others and sued them in court. They hoarded their wealth, refused to pay their workers, and condemned and murdered innocent men. The rich even slandered the name of Jesus. James advised rich people to weep and wail because misery would come upon them.

Noted Israeli botanist, Michael Zohary,[9] proposed that the wild flower identified by James was the crown daisy *(Chrysanthemum coronarium)*. Crown daisies grow in every region of Israel. Petals are yellow. Young leaves, stems, and flowers are used in salads and cooking recipes. The leaves are used as an expectorant and to ease stomach disorders.

In Latin, the language used to name plants, *coronarium* means "crown" in the sense of garland. In the ancient world, garlands were given to athletes who won competitions and conquerors successful in military battles. Today, children and young lovers place daisy chains around foreheads and necks.

The Bible has a lot to say about crowns. Almost 40 verses identify crowns or being crowned. The author of Proverbs wrote that wisdom will set a garland of grace on your head and present you with a crown of life (Pr 4:9). St. Peter noted that when the Chief Shepherd comes again, Christians will receive a crown (1 Pe 5:4). Always specific, James declared that the person who perseveres under trials will receive a crown of life (Jas 1:12). In Revelation, Jesus said that he was coming soon. He encouraged the faithful to hold on to their salvation so no one would take their crown from them (Rev 3:11).

For both rich and poor, men and women, life on earth ends. Ideally, all persevere under trials so that a crown will wait for them in the next life. At the same time, it is God and his son who deserve every crown because they created and redeemed us. Whatever we do to receive a crown is insignificant when compared to what God has done for us.

Reflection: Man is born and dies, riches are gained and lost, stars burst forth into the cosmos and die back to nothing, but our crown of glory from Jesus never fades away.

Perishable Field Flowers (1 Peter 1:22-25)

The author of First Peter was the apostle Peter. Peter wrote this letter in about 62–63 BC from Rome during the reign of the capricious Emperor Nero. Peter wrote to Gentiles scattered throughout the region that now encompass Asia Minor. Peter encouraged Christian believers to persevere in faith despite persecution. Christian's belief and hope is that they will enjoy end-time salvation.

The passage that depicted a flower blossom falling to the ground began with Peter reminding his readers that they have been born again, not with perishable, but with imperishable seed. The imperishable seed is the living and abiding Word of God, that is Jesus Christ. As a further reminder, Peter cited Isaiah who wrote that all flesh is like grass and the glory of flesh like flowers among grass (Isa 40:6-8). The grass withers and the flower falls, but the word of the Lord remains forever. Peter contrasted the weakness of human flesh with the power of the Word of God who grants new life to believers.

The flower referred to in 1 Peter was most likely the *Papaver rhoeas*, known as the common poppy and corn poppy.[9] The common poppy is short-lived. Petals unfold from the bud and last one-to-three days before dropping. Corn poppies are often red, but can be shades of pink. Each poppy has six-to-eight-petals. Poppies are so prevalent, that some agriculturalists in Israel consider them weeds.

The symbolism of St. Peter's flower is both perishable and imperishable. The poppy flower itself is perishable as is mankind's physical life. Our average life span in the West is around 80 years; while in some African nations, life span is less than 40 years. Whether 40 or 80 years, this life span is short when compared to inestimable eternity. A life of 40-80 years is but a blink of an eye in God's time frame.

Although our perishable bodies are short lived, God knows every second of those lives. God hurts when we hurt and rejoices when we rejoice. Constantly, God encourages us to make good decisions so we will be happy in this transient life.

Reflection: Have you ever thought about why God hates sin? God hates sin because of what it does to us, his children.

DESTRUCTION BY WORMWOOD (REVELATION 8:1-11)

St. John, the Beloved Disciple, is credited with writing Revelation. Revelation is an unveiling of spiritual forces operating behind the scenes in history. Revelation is largely prophecy, describing what will occur in the future, including the end-times.

In Revelation chapter eight, John described a vision in which he saw seven angels, each with a trumpet. These angels warned humanity of coming destruction and entreated them to repent. When the third trumpet sounded, a blazing star fell to earth. The star was named Wormwood.

When asteroids enter the earth's atmosphere and start to burn, children call them shooting stars. If a large asteroid hits the earth's surface, a huge dust cloud rises. The dust and particulates in the cloud spread around the globe, moved by winds and the rotation of the earth. Wormwood will contain a contaminant or release pollutants from the earth's surface that turned one-third of the earth's fresh water bitter.

The plant wormwood (*artemisia*) includes about 400 different species. The earliest description is in an Egyptian papyrus dated around 1600 BC. Wormwood was used to treat intestinal worms. Traditionally, wormwood flowers were love charms. An addictive drink, absinthe, is made from the leaves and flower tops of some species. Because it can cause convulsions and death, absinthe is illegal in some countries. Judean artemisia (*Artemisia judaica*) grows in Israel. Some artemisia plants are bright green, while others are muted gray-green. Most die back in the winter and regrow in spring. They are perennials.

In the Old Testament, wormwood was used as a metaphor for idolatry, calamity, sorrow, and false judgments. In Revelation, the star's name implied judgment for man's idolatry and injustice. In biblical times, idolatry referred to worship of idols, i.e., Baal, Artemis. Most Westerners don't worship statues or idols, but many are still idolaters. As I studied idolatry, I learned that it is an immoderate attachment or devotion to something. For some reason, I thought that idolatry was blind or excessive devotion to something.Immoderate means "exceeds usual or suitable bounds." Immoderate is a less extreme response than excess.

Reflection: Are any of your attachments immoderate? Is it time to realign your attachments to reflect what God wants them to be? How can you do this?

CINNAMON, A VALUABLE COMMODITY (REVELATION CHAPTER 18)

Because John wrote Revelation under the direction of the Holy Spirit, his writings could refer to world systems which operate in the future. From this perspective, Revelation 18 could predict a future collapse of the world commercial-economic systems. John prophesied that when commerce failed, there would be no cargoes of cinnamon and spice.

Most of us could get along without spices. It is difficult to imagine why cinnamon was mentioned in a list of valuable cargo items. Yet, in the first century the cinnamon trade was huge. The market price for an Egyptian pound (350 grams) of cinnamon was over 1,000 denarii. The typical Judean laborer worked about 3.2 years to earn 1,000 denarii. Ancient people used cinnamon for rituals, medicine, perfume, and cooking. Egyptians used cinnamon in embalming potions. Israelites included it as an ingredient in anointing oil. Cinnamon was used to reduce inflammation, promote menstruation, and stimulate the urinary tract.

The Bible cinnamon (*Cinnamomum zeylanicum*) came from aromatic tree bark. Arab traders brought cinnamon from the Far East to Mediterranean countries. The cinnamon tree doesn't grow naturally in Israel; however, the Jerusalem Botanical Garden has small cinnamon trees in its Conservatory.

Cinnamon is the quint-essential spice. Ask individuals to name a spice and most will name cinnamon. The archaic meaning of spice is a small portion or quantity, a dash, or something that gives zest to food or life. In the end times cinnamon will be unavailable. This dash or bit of zest will be absented from our lives.

We Christians may or may not be in the world when commerce and economic systems fail; however, to Christians having or not having cinnamon, luxury items, or even necessities aren't as important as having Jesus (Mt 6:33). Jesus isn't just a small portion, or dash, of spice in a Christian's life. Jesus is our world view. We need to set our mind on him (Col 3:1-2).

Reflection: Have you ever thought what your life would be like without God? Are you willing to giving God more space in your life?

THE GIFT OF DEATH (REVELATION 18:13)

John listed myrrh as a trade commodity no one would buy after Rome fell. The myrrh plant is the last plant in *Rooted in God 2;* yet, references to myrrh occurred from Genesis through Revelation. Joseph was sold to Ishmaelites who carried myrrh in trade caravans. Myrrh was a component of the Tabernacle anointing oil. Before she was taken to King Ahasaurus, Esther completed a twelve-month beauty treatment with myrrh. Myrrh was mentioned seven times in Song of Songs to describe the Lover, the Beloved, and Solomon's gardens.

In the ancient world, a variety of plant species were used to make myrrh. Likely, the Old Testament myrrh was from a different plant than the New Testament myrrh. In Imperial Rome, most myrrh came from the *Commiphora myrrha* plant; however, in Israel the *Commiphora abyssianica* was used to make myrrh. Arguably, John thought of Judean myrrh when he referred to myrrh in Revelation.

In present day Israel, myrrh trees grow in the Biblical Landscape Reserve. Although often called a spice, myrrh is a dried resin. When the resin is harvested, lateral cuts are made on the tree's trunk or branches. Gum resin exudes from the tree's wounds. Exposed to the air, the resin hardens forming irregular-shaped yellow or brown globules. Globules smell pleasant. Currently, myrrh is sold in the market in old city Jerusalem. The myrrh is broken into sharp-edged, marble-size, yellow-brown pieces.

Traditionally, myrrh symbolized both gifts and death. Wise men presented the Christ child with gifts of gold, frankincense, and myrrh. Following his death, Joseph of Arimathea and Nicodemus wrapped Jesus' body in linen perfumed with about 75 pounds of myrrh and aloes.

The original gifts—animals, food, drink—that Israelites brought to the Tabernacle and Temples couldn't clear the conscience of worshippers. Although the gifts met Tabernacle and Temple regulations, they were externals used until the new order came. The new order was the result of God's ultimate gift—his son sacrificed on the cross for your sins and my sins.

New Testament writers couldn't seem to focus on anyone but Jesus. I am sure that was God's intention. In a parallel way, Jesus should be the focus of a Christian's life. In Church on Sunday, we pray: "remembering Christ's life, death and resurrection, we await His Second Coming." Because we have the gift of Jesus Christ, we can wait with expectation and peace.

Reflection: Have you ever been embarrassed by a gift and not want to claim it? What is your response to the ultimate gift from God—the gift of his son?

Unifying Thoughts

Plants propagate and so did the early church. Propagation means to continue or to increase; it also means to pass along to the offspring. When we read about the early Christian church in Acts and in New Testament letters, we rejoice. Despite the hard times experienced by early church fathers, they passionately propagated "The Way" advocated by Jesus. Seemingly, nothing could stand against them.

Two millennia after Jesus' death, his followers face the same problems and persecutions as believers in early churches. Christians are a minority in society. Power, prestige, and money are the new idols. Immorality seems more relevant than Christian values.

1. Who were the first-century church members? What were their roles and occupations in life?

2. Name three places/settings where Jesus' followers propagated the message of Jesus as Savior of the world.

3. How can we, who are living in the twenty-first century, be like early church members and propagate the faith?

4. How often do you talk about Jesus and your belief that he is your Savior? Circle the time frame: monthly, weekly, daily. Are you happy with this frequency? Do you think it mirrors the frequency that early church members shared their faith?

5. Consider memorizing, then ask yourself who was Jesus talking to when he gave this directive: "Go into all the world and preach the good news to all creation" (Mk 16:15 niv).

PLANT PHOTOGRAPHS AND PHOTOGRAPHERS

Chapter	Plant	Photographer
1	Bdellium	Bart T. Wursten
1	Fig tree	Carolyn A. Roth
1	Milk thistle	Carolyn A. Roth
2	Cypress tree	Carolyn A. Roth
2	Mandrake	Sara Gold
2	Egyptian reed	Carolyn A. Roth
3	Blackberry bush	Carolyn A. Roth
3	Mangrove tree leaf	Peripitus,2012
4	Flax flower	Carolyn A. Roth
4	Almond tree	Carolyn A. Roth
4	Olive tree	Carolyn A. Roth
5	Henbane	Sara Gold
5	Date palm tree	Carolyn A. Roth
5	Yitran plant	Sara Gold
6	Pomegranate tree	Carolyn A. Roth
6	Terebinth flower	Yehiam Salts
6	Broad bean flower	Carolyn A. Roth
7	Henna plant	Carolyn A. Roth
7	Cedar tree	Carolyn A. Roth
7	Algum, almug	Karl Holtry
8	Broom tree, white	Carolyn A. Roth
8	Star of Bethlehem	Luigi Rignanese
8	Castor bean vine	Carolyn A. Roth
9	Apricot tree	Apple2008

9	Styrax tree	Carolyn A. Roth
9	Nettle plant	Luigi Rignanese
10	Goodly fruit	Carolyn A. Roth
10	Myrtle tree flower	Carolyn A. Roth
10	Cotton flower	Carolyn A. Roth
11	Frankincense	Carolyn A. Roth
11	Lily of the field, anemone	Carolyn A. Roth
11	Mustard tree	Sara Gold
12	Carob pods	Carolyn A. Roth
12	Mulberry tree	Luigi Rignanese
12	Nard, spikenard (American)	Carolyn A. Roth
13	Jerusalem thorn	Carolyn A. Roth
13	Opium poppy	Luigi Rignanese
13	Redbud tree	Greg Hume
14	Wormwood	Carolyn A. Roth
14	Myrrh	Carolyn A. Roth

REFERENCE LIST

1. Strong, James. *The New Strong's exhaustive concordance of the Bible.* Nashville, TN: Thomas Nelson Publishers, 2010.

2. Worcester, John. *Correspondences of the Bible: The plants.* West Chester, PA: Swedenborg Foundation Publishers, 2009.

3. Hareuveni, Nogah, and Helen Frenkley. *Tree and shrubs in our Biblical heritage.* Kiryat Ono, Israel: Neot Kedumim Limited, 1989.

4. Rabinowitz, Louis I. *Torah and flora.* New York, NY: Sanhedrin Press, 1977.

5. Walker, Winifred. *All the plants of the Bible.* Garden City, NY: Doubleday & Company, Incorporated, 1979.

6. Duke, James A., Peggy-Ann K. Duke, and Judith L. duCellier. *Duke's handbook of medicinal plants of the Bible.* Boca Raton, FL: CRC Press, Taylor & Francis Group, 2008.

7. Moldenke, Harold N., and Alma L. Moldenke. *Plants of the Bible.* Mineola, NY: Dover Publications, Incorporated, 1952.

8. MacDonald, William. *Believer's Bible commentary.* Nashville, TN: Thomas Nelson Publishers, 1995.

9. Zohary, Michael. *Plants of the Bible: A complete handbook.* New York, NY: Cambridge University Press, 1982.

Made in the USA
Columbia, SC
24 March 2020